RAINBOW IN THE SKY

JOHN GILPIN'S RIDE

Rainbow in the Sky

COLLECTED AND EDITED BY

LOUIS UNTERMEYER

ILLUSTRATED BY REGINALD BIRCH

HARCOURT BRACE JOVANOVICH, PUBLISHERS

SAN DIEGO   NEW YORK   LONDON

Printed in the United States of America

LIBRARY OF CONGRESS CATALOGING IN PUBLICATION DATA
Main entry under title:

Rainbow in the sky.

Summary: An anthology of over 500 poems primarily
by American and English writers, including Keats,
Longfellow, Robert Louis Stevenson, and David McCord.
1. Children's poetry, English.   2. Children's poetry, American.
[1. Poetry—Collections]
I. Untermeyer, Louis, 1885–1977.
I. Birch, Reginald Bathurst, 1856–1943, ill.
PR1175.3.R35   1985   821'.008'09282   84-19306
ISBN 0-15-265479-8

Golden Anniversary Edition

ABCDE

Typography by Robert Josephy

THIS BOOK

FOR ALL HAPPY CHILDREN

AND ESPECIALLY FOR ESTHER

(THE HAPPIEST *AND MOST CHILD-HEARTED OF THEM ALL)*

WHO HELPED ME MAKE IT

CONTENTS

Contents

Contents

THE FARMER IN THE DELL

BOYS AND GIRLS

Contents

RIDDLES IN RHYME

WINDS, WEATHERS, SEASONS, CHARMS

Contents

IN HEAVEN AND EARTH

FIN, FUR, AND FEATHER

Contents

"I'LL TELL YOU A STORY"

CAP AND BELLS

Contents

SIMPLY NONSENSE

THE ROAD TO ANYWHERE

OLD SONGS TO SING

Contents

HUSH-A-BY

TRUE ARROWS

Contents

xxiii

A WORD WITH YOU

Once upon a time there was a Flood. The rain fell for forty days, the rivers ran wild, the seas came up over the land. The fountains of the great deep broke out of the ground, and the windows of heaven were opened. Water was everywhere; no earth could be seen; even the mountain-tops were covered. All the people perished—all except a few that were in a great wooden Ark. Only Noah and his family and the animals that were with him remained alive, floating about in the Ark he had built. After a hundred and fifty days the waters began to go down, the sea returned to its proper place, and the Ark rested on a mountain called Ararat. Great were the rejoicings of Noah and his family and all the animals that were with him as they trooped out of the Ark. And just as they set their feet on dry land, a rainbow appeared in the sky. The rainbow glowed and glistened across the heavens, and God said it was a sign that they were rescued. He also said that it was a promise that the waters would never again flood the land and that the earth would be fair and fruitful forever.

Thousands of years after that there was a king. His enemies had captured him and put him in a tall tower, and no one knew where he had been hidden. For a while his friends searched for him, but, when time passed and there was no sign of him, they gave up the search—all except one man. This man had been the king's singer; wherever the king went, he carried the songs of his minstrel in his heart. All over Europe the singer went, singing in taverns, beside castle walls, under prison windows, singing and searching. One day he came to a tall tower heavily guarded.

"Away with you!" cried one of the soldiers. "We make short work of spies!"

"But I only wanted to sing you a song," replied the minstrel.

"Let him alone," said the captain. "He's not armed. A song can't do any harm to anyone—and it can't help anyone, either."

Saved
by
a
Song

A Word with You

So the minstrel sang. And high up in the tower, the king heard the song. He recognized the words, recognized the singer, too; and when the minstrel stopped, the king sang the second verse. Fortunately, the guards were rather deaf.

Now, at last, the singer knew where the king was hidden. He returned home to England, told the king's friends of his discovery, and a force was raised which soon rescued the noble prisoner.

"Saved by my faithful minstrel!" cried the king as he set foot on free earth.

"No, your majesty," replied the singer. "Saved by a song."

Poetry is many things. It is sometimes a jingle, or a dancing tune; sometimes it is a heroic tale, and sometimes nothing more than a merry measure, shaking its bells of rhyme. And it is sometimes an arrow in the air—a true arrow which, according to one poet, falls to earth in the most unexpected places. And it is often something that may rescue people from all sorts of cares and prisons.

But poetry is, first of all, a rainbow in the sky—a rainbow glowing with promise for everyone who will look, delighting the eye and uplifting the heart. It was on a rainbow that the gods of the North entered into their heaven; and it is at the end of the rainbow that there may be found the fabled pot of gold. And the arrow that points toward it, and the colored arc, and the bright path across the heaven, and the pot of gold itself are all one.

Open the book and see.

L. U.

JINGLES OLD AND NEW

JINGLES OLD AND NEW

Here are jingles, catches, and tunes—rhymes that are sensible and rhymes without reason. You have heard some of them before—you must have seen several in your first Mother Goose book—but there are many that will be new to you. The verses from "Sing-Song" were written by a famous poet, who was also the sister of a poet, both of whom lived and died in England many years ago. The rhymes from "Funday" and "Father Gander" are by a living poet who, when he is not drawing pictures to go with his jingles, is a New York lawyer.

The counting-out rhymes and the game-jingles have been heard all over America and England; some of them have been echoed even in Africa and Australia. Wherever boys and girls have skipped rope, bounced balls, joined hands in a circle, or taken sides in a tug-of-war these little verses have been sung. They were used many years ago by our grandparents; they can be heard today, especially during the long summer evenings, along dusky lanes, in village squares, in the streets of cities as far apart as Salem, Savannah, San Francisco, and the many Springfields throughout the United States.

Some of the names in "Important People" are the names of real persons. The Charley who loved a pretty girl as well as "good ale and wine" is the Prince Charles who fought so hard to recover his father's throne. You can find him in the English history books along with the Prince of Orange, Hector Protector, Edward the Confessor, and good King Arthur. King Arthur was the one who founded the famous Round Table where all his Knights dined, though history says nothing about bag-pudding being served at the court dinners. It is said that when another King, King Alfred, was hiding in disguise, he let some cakes burn and the countrywoman boxed his ears for being careless. At any rate (according to the rhyme) King Arthur taught *his* wife, whose name was Guinevere, not to be wasteful, for the poem tells us all the leftovers the thrifty queen "next morning fried." Georgey Porgey, whom you will find in the sec-

3

tion "Girls and Boys," may have been the pudgy George, who came over from Germany to be King of England, but I'm not sure. And I can't find any record of my favorite king of all kings, the happy, healthy, music-loving Old King Cole.

Some of the other important people are real people and lived not so long ago. Christopher Wrenn was a great architect and, as the rhyme tells you, built the cathedral of St. Paul in London. The Abbé Liszt, whose first name was Franz and who was born in Hungary, was one of the world's greatest pianists and is known for his rhapsodies and other pieces of music. Alfred de Musset was a French poet. Andrew Jackson was a great soldier and the seventh president of the United States. I don't have to tell you who Solomon and David were.

I haven't discovered anything about Simple Simon, Doctor Foster, Taffy, Solomon Grundy, or Bobby Shaftoe. Maybe they lived; maybe they didn't.

JUST JINGLES

Deedle, deedle, dumpling, my son John
Went to bed with his stockings on;
One shoe off, the other shoe on,
Deedle, deedle, dumpling, my son John.

To market, to market, to buy a fat pig;
Home again, home again, dancing a jig.
To market, to market, to buy a fat hog;
Home again, home again, jiggety jog.

Hey! diddle, diddle!
The cat and the fiddle;
The cow jumped over the moon.
The little dog laughed
To see such sport,
While the dish ran away with the spoon.

Cock-a-doodle-do!
My dame has lost her shoe;
My master's lost his fiddling stick
And doesn't know what to do.

Cock-a-doodle-do!
What is my dame to do?
Till master finds his fiddling stick,
She'll dance without her shoe.

Handy Spandy, Jack-a-dandy,
Loved plum-cake and sugar-candy.
He bought some at a grocer's shop
And out he came, hop, hop, hop.

Fiddle-de-dee, fiddle-de-dee,
The fly shall marry the bumble-bee.
They went to church, and married was she:
The fly has married the bumble-bee.

Old Mother Witch,
Couldn't sew a stitch,
Picked up a penny
And thought she was rich.

There was a piper, he had a cow.
And had no hay to give her;
He took his pipes and played a tune:
"Consider, old cow, consider!"

The cow considered very well,
For she gave the piper a penny
That he might play the tune again
Of "Corn rigs are bonnie."

Rub-a-dub-dub,
Three men in a tub:
And who do you think they be?
The butcher, the baker,
The candlestick-maker,
So turn 'em out, all three!

Tweedle-dum and Tweedle-dee
Resolved to have a battle
For Tweedle-dum said Tweedle-dee
Had spoiled his nice new rattle.

Just then flew by a monstrous crow
As big as a tar-barrel,
Which frightened both the heroes so
They quite forgot their quarrel.

Mother, may I go out to swim?
Yes, my darling daughter;
Hang your clothes on a hickory limb,
But don't go near the water.

Hark! Hark! The dogs do bark!
  The beggars have come to town.
Some in rags, and some in jags,
  And some in velvet gowns.

9

There was an old woman who lived in a shoe;
She had so many children she didn't know what to do;
She gave them some broth without any bread;
She whipped them all soundly and put them to bed.

There was an old woman called Nothing-at-all,
Who lived in a dwelling exceedingly small;
A man stretched his mouth to its utmost extent,
And down at one gulp house and old woman went.

Jack, be nimble;
Jack, be quick;
Jack, jump over
The candlestick.

Barber, barber, shave a pig;
How many hairs will make a wig?
"Four-and-twenty, that's enough."
Give the barber a pinch of snuff.

Tumbling Jack goes clickety-clack,
Down the ladder and then comes back.
Clickety-clackety, rattle and hop,
Over and down again, flippety-flop!

Peter, Peter, pumpkin-eater,
Had a wife and couldn't keep her.
He put her in a pumpkin shell,
And there he kept her very well.

I'll tell you a story
About Jack o' Nory—
And now my story's begun.

I'll tell you another
About Johnny, his brother—
And now my story is done.

ONE

ONE MISTY MOISTY MORNING

One misty moisty morning,
    When cloudy was the weather,
I met a little old man
    Clothed all in leather;
He began to bow and scrape,
    And I began to grin—
How do you do, and how do you do,
    And how do you do again?

II

If all the world were apple-pie,
And all the sea were ink,
And all the trees were bread and cheese,
What should we have to drink?

There was a man of our town,
    And he was wondrous wise,
He jumped into a bramble bush,
    And scratched out both his eyes.

But when he saw his eyes were out,
    With all his might and main,
He jumped into another bush,
    And scratched 'em in again!

There was an owl lived in an oak;
    Whiskey, whaskey, wheedle.
And all the words he ever spoke
    Were fiddle, faddle, feedle.

A sportsman chanced to hear that word:
    Whiskey, whaskey, wheedle.
Said he, "I'll shoot you, silly bird!"
    So—fiddle, faddle, feedle.

Jack Hall,
He is so small,
A mouse could eat him,
Hat and all.

This little piggy went to market;
This little piggy stayed home;
This little piggy had roast beef;
This little piggy had none;
And this little piggy cried, "Wee! Wee! Wee!"
All the way home.

Five little squirrels
Sat in a tree.
The first one said,
"What do I see?"
The second one said,
"A man with a gun."
The third one said,
"We'd better run."
The fourth one said,
"Let's hide in the shade."
The fifth one said,
"*I'm* not afraid."
Then BANG went the gun,
And how they did run!

THE HOUSE THAT JACK BUILT

This is the house that Jack built.

This is the malt
That lay in the house that Jack built.

This is the rat,
That ate the malt,
That lay in the house that Jack built.

This is the cat,
That killed the rat,
That ate the malt,
That lay in the house that Jack built.

This is the dog,
That worried the cat,
That killed the rat,
That ate the malt,
That lay in the house that Jack built.

This is the cow with the crumpled horn,
That tossed the dog,
That worried the cat,
That killed the rat,
That ate the malt,
That lay in the house that Jack built.

This is the maiden all forlorn,
That milked the cow with the crumpled horn,
That tossed the dog,
That worried the cat,
That killed the rat,
That ate the malt,
That lay in the house that Jack built.

This is the man all tattered and torn,
That kissed the maiden all forlorn,
That milked the cow with the crumpled horn,
That tossed the dog,
That worried the cat,
That killed the rat,
That ate the malt,
That lay in the house that Jack built.

This is the priest all shaven and shorn,
That married the man all tattered and torn,
That kissed the maiden all forlorn,
That milked the cow with the crumpled horn,
That tossed the dog,
That worried the cat,
That killed the rat,
That ate the malt,
That lay in the house that Jack built.

This is the cock that crowed in the morn,
That waked the priest all shaven and shorn,
That married the man all tattered and torn,
That kissed the maiden all forlorn,
That milked the cow with the crumpled horn,
That tossed the dog,
That worried the cat,
That killed the rat,
That ate the malt,
That lay in the house that Jack built.

This is the farmer sowing his corn,
That kept the cock that crowed in the morn,
That waked the priest all shaven and shorn,
That married the man all tattered and torn,
That kissed the maiden all forlorn,
That milked the cow with the crumpled horn,
That tossed the dog,
That worried the cat,
That killed the rat,
That ate the malt,
That lay in the house that Jack built.

TEN LITTLE INJUNS

Ten little Injuns standing in a line—
One went home, and then there were nine.

Nine little Injuns swinging on a gate—
One tumbled off, and then there were eight.

Eight little Injuns tried to get to heaven—
One kicked the bucket, and then there were seven.

Seven little Injuns cutting up tricks—
One went to bed, and then there were six.

Six little Injuns learning how to dive—
One swam away, and then there were five.

Five little Injuns on a cellar door—
One jumped off, and then there were four.

Four little Injuns climbing up a tree—
One fell down, and then there were three.

Three little Injuns out in a canoe—
One fell overboard, and then there were two.

Two little Injuns fooling with a gun—
One shot the other, and then there was one.

One little Injun living all alone—
He got married, and then there was none!

IMPORTANT PEOPLE

Old King Cole
Was a merry old soul,
And a merry old soul was he.
He called for his pipe,
And he called for his bowl,
And he called for his fiddlers three.

Now every fiddler
He had a fiddle,
And a very fine fiddle had he;
O, there's none so rare
As can compare
With King Cole and his fiddlers three!

The King of France with fifty thousand men,
Marched up the hill and then marched down again.

Hector Protector was dressed all in green;
Hector Protector was sent to the Queen.
The Queen did not like him, no more did the King;
So Hector Protector was sent back again.

When good King Arthur ruled this land,
   He was a goodly king;
He stole three pecks of barley-meal,
   To make a bag-pudding.

A bag-pudding the king did make,
   And stuffed it well with plums;
And in it put great lumps of fat,
   As big as my two thumbs.

The king and queen did eat thereof,
    And noblemen beside;
And what they could not eat that night,
    The queen next morning fried.

What is the rhyme for *porringer*?
The King he had a daughter fair,
And gave the Prince of Orange her.

Over the water, and over the sea,
And over the water to Charley;
Charley loves good ale and wine,
And Charley loves good brandy,
And Charley loves a pretty girl,
As sweet as sugar-candy.

Over the water and over the sea,
And over the water to Charley;
I'll have none of your nasty beef,
Nor I'll have none of your barley;
But I'll have some of your very best flour,
To make a white cake for my Charley.

As I was going by Charing Cross,
I saw a black man upon a black horse;
They told me it was King Charles the First.
Oh, dear! my heart was ready to burst!

Poor old Robinson Crusoe,
Poor old Robinson Crusoe,
 They made him a coat
 Of an old nanny goat,
I wonder how they could do so.

Poor old Robinson Crusoe,
Poor old Robinson Crusoe,
 When he went for a nap
 He took off his cap,
Because his own hair grew so.

Robin and Richard were two pretty men;
They lay in bed till the clock struck ten;
Then up starts Robin and looks at the sky,
"Oh! brother Richard, the sun's very high:

The bull's in the barn threshing the corn,
The cock's on the dunghill blowing his horn,
The cat's at the fire frying of fish,
The dog's in the pantry breaking his dish."

Washington, man of mystery,
Fought till his hands grew blistery.
 He froze his toes,
 Likewise his nose,
But smiled. The rest is history.

Simple Simon met a pieman,
   Going to the fair;
Says Simple Simon to the pieman,
   "Let me taste your ware."

Says the pieman to Simple Simon,
   "Show me first your penny."
Says Simple Simon to the pieman,
   "Indeed, I have not any."

Simple Simon went a-fishing
   For to catch a whale:
All the water he had got
   Was in his mother's pail!

25

Doctor Foster went to Glo'ster
 In a shower of rain;
He stepped in a puddle, up to his middle,
 And never went there again.

Old Mother Goose, when
She wanted to wander,
Would ride through the air
On a very fine gander.

Mother Goose had a house,
'Twas built in a wood,
Where an owl at the door
For sentinel stood.

In a cottage in Fife
Lived a man and his wife
Who, believe me, were comical folk;
 For to people's surprise,
 They both saw with their eyes,
And their tongues moved whenever they spoke.

When they were asleep
(I'm told) that to keep
Their eyes open they could not contrive;
 They both walked on their feet;
 And whate'er they did eat,
Helped, with drinking, to keep them alive.

Taffy was a Welshman, Taffy was a thief;
Taffy came to my house and stole a piece of beef:
I went to Taffy's house, Taffy was not at home;
Taffy came to my house and stole a marrow-bone.

I went to Taffy's house, Taffy was not in;
Taffy came to my house and stole a silver pin:
I went to Taffy's house, Taffy was in bed,
I took up a poker and flung it at his head.

Little Jack Horner sat in a corner,
  Eating a Christmas pie;
He put in his thumb, and pulled out a plum,
  And said, "What a good boy am I!"

Solomon Grundy,
Born on a Monday,
Christened on Tuesday,
Married on Wednesday,
Took ill on Thursday,
Worse on Friday,
Died on Saturday,
Buried on Sunday:
This is the end
Of Solomon Grundy.

Old Mother Hubbard
Went to the cupboard
   To get her poor dog a bone;
But when she got there
The cupboard was bare,
   And so the poor dog had none.

She went to the baker's
   To buy him some bread,
But when she came back
   The poor dog was dead.

She went to the joiner's
   To buy him a coffin,
But when she came back
   The poor dog was laughing.

She took a clean dish
   To get him some tripe,
But when she came back
   He was smoking his pipe.

She went to the fish-man's
   To buy him some fish,
And when she came back
   He was licking the dish.

She went to the ale-house
   To get him some beer,
But when she came back
   The dog sat in a chair.

She went to the tavern
   For white-wine and red,
But when she came back
   The dog stood on his head.

BUT WHEN SHE GOT THERE THE CUPBOARD WAS BARE

She went to the hatter's
  To buy him a hat,
But when she came back
  He was feeding the cat.

She went to the barber's
  To buy him a wig,
But when she came back
  He was dancing a jig.

She went to the fruiterer's
  To buy him some fruit,
But when she came back
  He was playing the flute.

She went to the tailor's
  To buy him a coat,
But when she came back
  He was riding a goat.

She went to the cobbler's
  To buy him some shoes,
But when she came back
  He was reading the news.

She went to the seamstress
  To buy him some linen,
But when she came back
  The dog was spinning.

She went to the hosier's
  To buy him some hose,
But when she came back
  He was dressed in his clothes.

The dame made a curtsey,
  The dog made a bow;
The dame said, "Your servant,"
  The dog said, "Bow wow."

Bobby Shaftoe's gone to sea,
Silver buckles at his knee,
When he comes back he'll marry me;
    Bonny Bobby Shaftoe.

Bobby Shaftoe's fat and fair,
Bright blue eyes and golden hair;
He's my love for evermair,
    Bonny Bobby Shaftoe.

The Queen of Hearts
She made some tarts
All on a summer's day;
    The Knave of Hearts
He stole those tarts,
And with them ran away.

The King of Hearts
Called for the tarts,
And beat the knave full sore;
    The Knave of Hearts
Brought back the tarts,
And vowed he'd steal no more.

Edward the Confessor
Slept under the dresser.
When that began to pall,
He slept out in the hall.

The Abbé Liszt
Banged the piano with his fist.
That was the way
He liked to play!

Andrew Jackson
Was an Anglo-Saxon
Who lived on pork and beans.
When tired of that,
He lived on fat
Hog-jowl and greens.

Said Sir Christopher Wrenn,
"I'm going to dine with some men.
If anybody calls,
Say I'm designing St. Paul's."

King Solomon and King David
And their forty-'leven wives
Raised Cain in old Jerusalem,
And lived ungodly lives.

But when old age came on them
With all its many qualms,
King Solomon took to Proverbs,
And David wrote the Psalms.

Alfred de Musset
Used to call his cat "Pussé."
His accent was affected.
That was to be expected.

I do not love thee, Doctor Fell;
The reason why I cannot tell.
But this I know, and know full well,
I do not love thee, Doctor Fell.

RHYMES FOR A CHARM

Kitty, Kitty,
Wash your paws,
And draw back all
Your shining claws!
Purr you shall,
And growl you shan't,
Or you'll get something
You don't want!

The dog barks,
The cat mews,
The mule goes nowhere
He does not choose,
And far away
A lion roars—
And people are glad
They shut the doors.

33

You play a fife,
And I'll play a drum.
If we play long enough
An ogre will come,
An ogre, a dragon, and a blind man—
Run about, spin about, catch as catch can!

ELIZABETH COATSWORTH

COUNTING-OUT RHYMES

Hickory, dickory, dock,
The mouse ran up the clock.
    The clock struck one,
    The mouse ran down,
And O U T spells OUT!

Eenie, meenie, miney, mo;
Catch a piggy by the toe.
If he hollers let him go.
Eenie, meenie, miney, mo.

One-ery, Ore-ery, Ickery, Ann,
Phillip-son, Phollop-son, Nicholas, John,
    Queevy, Quavy,
    English Navy,
Zinglum, Zanglum, Bolum, Bun.

Monkey, monkey, bottle of beer;
How many monkeys have we here?
One Two Three Four. . . .
That is all unless there's more.

Engine, engine, number nine,
Sliding down Chicago line;
When she's polished she will shine,
Engine, engine, number nine.

Ibbity, bibbity, sibbity, sab,
Ibbity, bibbity, canal-boat.
   Dictionary;
   Down the ferry;
   Fun! Fun!
   American gun!
Eighteen hundred and sixty-one!

One, two, three,
The Bumble-Bee.
The Rooster crows,
And up he goes!

One, two, three, four, five, six, seven,
All good children go to heaven.
   When they die,
   Mothers cry;
One, two, three, four, five, six, seven.

Icker-backer,
Soda cracker,
Icker-backer-boo.
En-gine
Number nine,
Out go y-o-u!

Wire, briar, limber-lock,
Three geese in a flock;
One flew east, one flew west,
And one flew over the cuckoo's nest.

GAMES

Down the market,
Down the sea,
Down the ocean,
One, two, three.

A tisket, a tasket,
A green and yellow basket;
I wrote a letter to my love,
And on the way I dropped it,
I dropped it.
Along came a little boy
And put it in his pocket,
his pocket.
Was it you? Was it you? Was it you?

Water, water, wild-flower,
Growing up so high,
We are all young ladies,
And we are sure to die,
Excepting little Mary,
She is the fairest flower.
Wild-flower, wild-flower, show your shame,
Turn your back and tell your sweetheart's name.

Robert, Robert, is a nice young man;
He comes to the door with his hat in his hand.
Down comes she all dressed in white,
Tomorrow, tomorrow, the wedding shall begin.
Doctor, doctor, can you tell
What will make poor Mary well?
For she is sick and ready to die,
And that will make poor Robert cry.

The farmer in the dell,
The farmer in the dell,
Heigh-ho, the dairy-oh,
The farmer in the dell.

The wife takes a child,
The wife takes a child,
Heigh-ho, the dairy-oh,
The wife takes a child.

The farmer takes a wife,
The farmer takes a wife,
Heigh-ho, the dairy-oh,
The farmer takes a wife.

The child takes a dog,
The child takes a dog,
Heigh-ho, the dairy-oh,
The child takes a dog.

The dog claps out,
The dog claps out,
Heigh-ho, the dairy-oh,
The dog claps out.

Strolling on the green grass,
      green grass,
      green grass,
Strolling on the green grass,
A husky, dusky day.

Who are you going to marry,
      marry,
      marry?

Who are you going to marry?
A husky, dusky day.

I am going to marry Jimmie,
      Jimmie,
      Jimmie,
I am going to marry Jimmie,
A husky, dusky day.

Oats, peas, beans and barley grow,
Oats, peas, beans and barley grow,
Not you nor I nor anyone knows
How oats, peas, beans and barley grow.

First the farmer sows the seeds,
Then he stands and takes his ease,
He stamps his foot, and claps his hand,
And turns around to view the land.

Waiting for a partner,
Waiting for a partner,
Open the ring and let one in,
And then we'll dance and gayly sing:

Oats, peas, beans and barley grow,
Oats, peas, beans and barley grow,
Not you nor I nor anyone knows
How oats, peas, beans and barley grow.

Now you're married you must obey;
You must be true to all you say;
You must be kind, you must be good,
And keep your wife in kindling wood.

POP GOES THE WEASEL

A penny for a ball of thread,
Another for a needle.
That's the way the money goes;
   Pop goes the Weasel!

All around the cobbler's bench,
The monkey chased the people;
The donkey thought 'twas all in fun.
   Pop goes the Weasel!

Queen Victoria's very sick;
Napoleon's got the measles;
Sally's got the whooping cough;
   Pop goes the Weasel!

Of all the dances ever planned,
To fling the heel and fly the hand,
There's none that moves so gay and grand
   As Pop goes the Weasel!

The lover, when he pants through fear
To pop the question to his dear,
He joins this dance, then in his ear
   Pop goes the Weasel!

A penny for a ball of thread,
Another for a needle.
That's the way the money goes;
   Pop goes the Weasel!

ALL AROUND THE MULBERRY BUSH

All around the mulberry bush,
        mulberry bush,
        mulberry bush,
All around the mulberry bush,
All on a Monday morning.

This is the way we wash our clothes,
        wash our clothes,
        wash our clothes.
This is the way we wash our clothes
All on a Monday morning.

This is the way we hang our clothes,
        hang our clothes,
        hang our clothes.
This is the way we hang our clothes
All on a Tuesday morning.

This is the way we sprinkle our clothes,
        sprinkle our clothes,
        sprinkle our clothes.
This is the way we sprinkle our clothes
All on a Wednesday morning.

This is the way we iron our clothes,
        iron our clothes,
        iron our clothes.
This is the way we iron our clothes
All on a Thursday morning.

This is the way we sweep our house,
        sweep our house,
        sweep our house.
This is the way we sweep our house
All on a Friday morning.

This is the way we take a walk,
         take a walk,
         take a walk.
This is the way we take a walk
All on a Saturday morning.

This is the way we go to church,
         go to church,
         go to church.
This is the way we go to church
All on a Sunday morning.

All around the mulberry bush,
*   mulberry bush,*
*   mulberry bush,*
All around the mulberry bush,
All on a Sunday morning.

EASY LESSONS

Thirty days hath September,
April, June, and November.
All the rest have thirty-one,
Except February alone,
Which has four and twenty-four
Till leap-year gives it one day more.

One, two,
Buckle my shoe;
Three, four,
Shut the door;
Five, six,
Pick up sticks;
Seven, eight,
Lay them straight;
Nine, ten,
A big fat hen;
Eleven, twelve,
Who will delve?
Thirteen, fourteen,
Maids-a-courting;
Fifteen, sixteen,
Maids-a-kissing;
Seventeen, eighteen,
Maids-a-waiting;
Nineteen, twenty,
My stomach's empty.

When V and I together meet,
They make the number Six complete.
When I with V do meet once more,
Then these two letters make but Four.
And when that V from I is gone,
Alas, poor I can make but One.

Columbus sailed the ocean blue
In Fourteen Hundred and Ninety-two.

Sixty seconds make a minute—
How much good can I do in it?
Sixty minutes make an hour—
All the good that's in my power.

Stop! Look! and Listen!
Before you cross the street.
Use your eyes; use your ears;
Then use your feet!

A B C D E F G,
H I J K L M N O P,
Q R S T U and V,
W X Y and Z.
Oh, how happy I shall be
When I've learned my A B C!

I before E
Except after C,
Or when sounded like A
As in "neighbor" or "weigh."

HARD LESSONS

Multiplication is vexation,
Division is as bad;
The Rule of Three it puzzles me,
And fractions drive me mad.

ANATOMY LESSON

My body is a poem,
My body's full of rhymes;
That is what I've thought about
Many, many times.

For I have toes,
A chin and nose,

Cheeks and lips,
Arms and hips,

Shoulders, thighs,
Brows and eyes,

Fingers, thumbs,
Ears and drums,

Throat and breast,
Knee and chest,

Tooth and tongue,
Heart and lung.

That is how I figured out
Many, many times,
My body is a poem
Because it's full of rhymes.

ILO ORLEANS

43

HISTORY LESSON

The Sovereigns of England

First, William the Norman,
Then William his son;
Henry, Stephen, and Henry,
Then Richard and John.
Next, Henry the third,
Edwards, one, two, and three;
And again, after Richard,
Three Henrys we see.
Two Edwards, third Richard,
If rightly I guess;
Two Henrys, sixth Edward,
Queen Mary, Queen Bess;
Then Jamie the Scotchman,
Then Charles whom they slew,
Yet received, after Cromwell,
Another Charles, too.
Next Jamie the second
Ascended the throne.
Then good William and Mary
Together came on;
Then Anne, Georges four,
And fourth William all passed,
And Victoria came—
Long did she last.
Next Edward the Seventh
Whose praises we sing;
Then our own George Fifth—
God save the King.

From "SING-SONG"

1

"Kookoorookoo! Kookoorookoo!"
  Crows the cock before the morn;
"Kikirikee! Kikirikee!"
  Roses in the east are born.

"Kookoorookoo! Kookoorookoo!"
  Early birds begin their singing;
"Kikirikee! Kikirikee!"
  The day, the day, the day is springing.

2

Eight o'clock;
The postman's knock!
Five letters for Papa;
  One for Lou,
  And none for you,
And three for dear Mamma.

3

Growing in the vale
  By the uplands hilly,
Growing straight and frail,
  Lady Daffadowndilly.

In a golden crown,
And a scant green gown,
  While the spring blows chilly,
Lady Daffadown,
  Sweet Daffadowndilly.

4

Brownie, Brownie, let down your milk,
White as swansdown and smooth as silk,
Fresh as dew and pure as snow:
For I know where the cowslips blow,
And you shall have a cowslip wreath
No sweeter scented than your breath.

5

The days are clear,
   Day after day,
When April's here,
   That leads to May,
And June
Must follow soon:
   Stay, June, stay!
If only we could stop the moon—
And June!

6

A pocket handkerchief to hem
   Oh dear, oh dear, oh dear!
How many stitches it will take
   Before it's done, I fear.

Yet set a stitch and then a stitch,
   And stitch and stitch away,
Till stitch by stitch the hem is done—
   And after work is play!

7

A pin has a head, but has no hair;
A clock has a face, but no mouth there;
Needles have eyes, but they cannot see;
A fly has a trunk without lock or key;
A timepiece may lose, but cannot win;
A corn-field dimples without a chin;
A hill has no leg, but has a foot;
A wine-glass a stem, but not a root;
Rivers run, though they have no feet;
A saw has teeth, but it does not eat;
Ash-trees have keys, yet never a lock;
And baby crows, without being a cock.

8

A motherless soft lambkin
  Alone upon a hill;
No mother's fleece to shelter him
  And wrap him from the cold:—
I'll run to him, and comfort him,
  I'll fetch him, that I will;
I'll care for him and feed him
  Until he's strong and bold.

9

Boats sail on the rivers,
    And ships sail on the seas;
But clouds that sail across the sky
    Are prettier far than these.

There are bridges on the rivers,
    As pretty as you please;
But the bow that bridges heaven,
    And overtops the trees,
And builds a road from earth to sky,
    Is prettier far than these.

10

Hurt no living thing:
    Ladybird, nor butterfly,
Nor moth with dusty wing,
    Nor cricket chirping cheerily,
Nor grasshopper so light of leap,
    Nor dancing gnat, nor beetle fat,
Nor harmless worms that creep.

11

What does the bee do?
    Bring him honey.
And what does father do?
    Bring him money.
And what does mother do?
    Lay out the money.
And what does baby do?
    Eat up the honey.

12

If stars dropped out of heaven,
    And if flowers took their place,
The sky would still look very fair,
    And fair earth's face.

Winged angels might fly down to us
    To pluck the stars,
But we could only long for flowers
    Beyond the cloudy bars.

CHRISTINA ROSSETTI

From "FATHER GANDER"

Little man,
   Little man,
How do you do?
How is your sock
And how is your shoe?

Little man,
   Little man,
How do you feel?
How is your sole
And how is your heel?

I saw a dog
Who wasn't a dog,
And a cat
Who wasn't a cat.
Of course, it was
In a dream I saw
Strange animals
   Like that.

With a camel's hump,
And an elephant's trunk,
And the neck of a tall giraffe,
And a fish's tail,
And the shell of a snail,
And the giggliest kind
   Of laugh.

49

Shoes have tongues,
But cannot talk;
Tables have legs,
But cannot walk;

Needles have eyes,
But cannot see;
Chairs have arms,
But they can't hug me!

Water has no color.
Snow is purest white.
    I wonder where
    The white all went
From the melting snow
    Last night.

Soap is green,
Or red, or white,
Or brown, or black
    As ink;
But when you wash
They all turn white!
That is so strange,
    I think.

I offered the donkey
Some ice-cream,
He turned up his nose
For, alas!

A donkey is only
A donkey,
And a donkey is always
An Ass!

The sky came tripping
Down to earth,
And this is how I know;
I walked about
The garden, and
I found these flowers grow:
The SUNflower and
The MOONflower and
The brilliant blazing STAR.
And since I found
Them there, I think,
The sky can't be so far!

ILO ORLEANS

From "FUNDAY"

Give me the sky
For a playground;

Give me the sun
For a ball;

Give me the rainbow
To skip with,

And I'll never be naughty
At all!

The clouds in the sky
Have the funniest shapes
    Of lions
    And tigers
    And panthers
    And apes.

They twist and they turn,
And they split into two.

I'm sure that in heaven
There must be a Zoo.

It isn't hard
To drive a car;
I'm sure that I
Can drive one far.

And if I only
Had a chance,
I'd travel out
To Greece or France.

For this is all
There is to know:
That Red means "Stop"
And Green means "Go."

Rainbow in the Sky

Upon the beach
With pail and spade,
My sandy pies and wells I made.

And people passed
On every hand
And left their footprints on the sand.

Then came a wave
With the rushing tide—
And everything was washed aside.

I thank you, God,
For a hundred things:
For the flower that blooms,
For the bird that sings,
For the sun that shines,
And the rain that drops,
For ice cream,
 and raisins,
 and lollypops.
 AMEN.

Soldiers fight by land and air,
And sailors fight by sea,
But I can think of other things
That I'd prefer to be.

I'd rather build a bridge or house,
I'd rather print a book,
I'd rather make a ship or plane,
I'd rather bake or cook.

I'd rather farm or hunt or fish,
I'd rather paint or write,
Than spend my days just waiting for
A chance to have a fight.

ILO ORLEANS

SPRING RING-JINGLE

Fol-de-rol and riddle-ma-ree,
Come and join my jubilee,
I'm the riddle and I'm the key,
I'm the robin up in the tree,
I'm the river that runs to sea,
I'm the flag that's flying free,
I'm the salmon that's on a spree,
I'm the faun that's taught to flee,
I'm the flower that's caught a bee,
I am all I ought to be—
For, when Spring sounds "revelry,"
I'm all these and they are me,
So I sing for very glee
Fol-de-rol and riddle-ma-ree.

MICHAEL LEWIS

53

MAKING MUSHROOMS

Larry and Gogo love mushrooms,
   But God didn't send any rain.
So Mother said, "Turn on the garden-hose . . ."
   Now we have mushrooms again!

                  ESTHER ANTIN

THE HOTTENTOT TOT

Through the street as I trot when the weather is hot,
Then I envy the lot of a Hottentot tot,
For he lies in the shade of a glade just arrayed
In the very same costume in which he was made.
   I'd be pinched on the spot
   If I so far forgot
   As to copy the style of
   The Hottentot tot.

Oh, the Hottentot tot, though you like him or not,
In his tropical grot he can teach us a lot;
For he cares not who stares at the costume he wears,
For his neighbors are natives and tigers and bears;
   And they do not care what
   He is wearing; the lot
   Are all dressed up the same as
   The Hottentot tot.

                  NEWMAN LEVY

WHEN I WAS CHRISTENED

When I was christened,
they held me up
and poured some water
out of a cup.

The trouble was
it fell on me,
and I and water
don't agree.

A lot of christeners
stood and listened.
I let them *know*
that I was christened!

DAVID MC CORD

THE FARMER IN THE DELL

THE FARMER IN THE DELL

Here, as you might guess from the heading, are verses about the farm and barnyard, about all the things that go on in the country, such as plowing, and planting, and milking, and calling the cows, and sheep-tending, and wool-gathering. Some of the verses in the first group—the ones about the black sheep, and the little pigs, and the fat hen, and Tom Tinker's dog, and the farmer's gray mare, and the three blind mice—have come out of Mother Goose's collection of tales, tunes and tinkles. But, though the verses may not be new, the arrangement is. You will find some old friends here and some strange faces, who (I hope) will soon be old friends.

I think a few of the new ones will surprise you. For instance, on page 76 you will find four favorite pieces from Robert Louis Stevenson's "A Child's Garden of Verses." (You will find more poems from that lovely collection elsewhere in this book.) And right next to it, on page 77, you will find the same verses twisted about a little so that these twists—called "parodies"—make you smile when you least expect to.

The last poem in this section, "The Harpers' Farm" by Dorothy Aldis, is a little like one in the next section, the one called "The Picnic" by Elizabeth Madox Roberts. Do you see the likeness—and the difference? And which, I wonder, do you like better?

FARM AND BARNYARD

Baa, baa, black sheep,
　　Have you any wool?
Yes, sir; yes, sir,
　　Three bags full.
One for my master,
　　One for my dame,
And one for the little boy
　　Who lives in the lane.

Higgledy Piggledy,
　　My fat hen,
She lays eggs
　　For gentlemen;
Sometimes nine,
　　And sometimes ten.
Higgledy Piggledy,
　　My fat hen.

Bow, wow, wow,
Who's dog art thou?
"Little Tom Tinker's dog,
Bow, wow, wow."

Little Boy Blue, come blow your horn,
The sheep's in the meadow, the cow's in the corn.
"Where is the boy that looks after the sheep?"
"He's under the hay-cock fast asleep."
"Will you awake him?" "No, not I;
For if I do, he'll be sure to cry."

Goosey, goosey, gander,
   Where shall I wander?
Up stairs, down stairs,
   And in my lady's chamber.
There I met an old man
   Who would not say his prayers;
I took him by the left leg
   And threw him down the stairs.

UNDER THE HAY-COCK FAST ASLEEP

A farmer went trotting
    Upon his gray mare;
Bumpety, bumpety, bump!
With his daughter behind him,
    So rosy and fair;
Lumpety, lumpety, lump!

A raven cried, "Croak;"
    And they all tumbled down;
Bumpety, bumpety, bump!
The mare broke her knees,
    And the farmer his crown;
Lumpety, lumpety, lump!

Some little mice sat in a barn to spin.
Pussy came by, and popped her head in.
"Shall I come in and cut your threads off?"
"Oh, no, kind sir, you will snap our heads off!"

Mistress Mary,
    Quite contrary,
How does your garden grow?
    With silver bells,
    And cockle shells,
And columbines all in a row.

Three blind mice, see how they run!
They all ran after the farmer's wife;
She cut off their tails with the carving-knife;
Did you ever see such a thing in your life
  As three blind mice?

My maid Mary
She minds her dairy,
  While I go a-hoeing and mowing each morn.

Merrily runs the reel
And the little spinning-wheel
  Whilst I am singing and mowing my corn.

AND CAN'T TELL WHERE TO FIND THEM

Little Bo-Peep has lost her sheep,
    And can't tell where to find them;
Leave them alone, and they'll come home,
    Wagging their tails behind them.

Little Bo-Peep fell fast asleep,
    And dreamt she heard them bleating;
But when she awoke, she found it a joke,
    For they were still a-fleeting.

SHE FOUND THEM INDEED

Then up she took her little crook,
  Determined for to find them;
She found them indeed, but it made her heart bleed,
  For they'd left all their tails behind 'em.

It happened one day, as Bo-Peep did stray
  Under a meadow hard by:
There she espied their tails side by side,
  All hung on a tree to dry.

SHOEING SONGS

Shoe the colt,
Shoe the colt,
Shoe the wild mare;
Here a nail,
There a nail,
Or she goes bare.

"Is John Smith within?"
"Yes, that he is."
"Can he set a shoe?"
"Aye, marry, two.
Here a nail, there a nail,
Tick, tack, too.

"Robert Barnes, fellow fine,
Can you shoe this horse of mine?"
"Yes, good sir, that I can,
As well as any other man:
There's a nail, and there's a prod,
And now, good sir, your horse is shod."

Cobbler, cobbler, mend my shoe;
Have it done by half-past two.
If by then it can't be done,
Have it done by half-past one.

THE USEFUL PLOW

A country life is sweet!
In moderate cold and heat,
   To walk in the air, how pleasant and fair,
In every field of wheat,
   The fairest of flowers adorning the bowers,
And every meadow's brow;
    So that I say, no courtier may
    Compare with them who clothe in gray,
And follow the useful plow.

They rise with the morning lark,
And labor till almost dark;
   Then folding their sheep, they hasten to sleep;
While every pleasant park
   Next morning is ringing with birds that are singing,
On each green tender bough.
    With what content and merriment,
    Their days are spent, whose minds are bent
To follow the useful plow!

THE JOLLY MILLER

There was a jolly miller
　　Lived on the river Dee;
He worked and sung from morn till night,
　　No lark as blithe as he;
And this the burden of his song
　　For ever used to be:
"I jump me jerrime jee!
　　I care for nobody—no! not I,
Since nobody cares for me."

ISAAC BICKERSTAFF

72

IN THE GARDEN

It's good to be back
   At the soil again,
Out in the garden
   To toil again.

It's good to plant
   And to sow again,
To dig and to rake
   And to hoe again.

I'm happy and merry:
   I sing again,
Because today
   It is Spring again.

ILO ORLEANS

MILKING TIME

When supper time is almost come,
But not quite here, I cannot wait,
And so I take my china mug
And go down by the milking gate.

The cow is always eating shucks
And spilling off the little silk.
Her purple eyes are big and soft—
She always smells like milk.

And father takes my mug from me,
And then he makes the stream come out.
I see it going in my mug
And foaming all about.

And when it's piling very high,
And when some little streams commence
To run and drip along the sides,
He hands it to me through the fence.

ELIZABETH MADOX ROBERTS

73

THE PRETTY MILKMAID

"Where are you going, my pretty maid?"
"I'm going a-milking, sir," she said.
"May I go with you, my pretty maid?"
"You're kindly welcome, sir," she said.
"What is your father, my pretty maid?"
"My father's a farmer, sir," she said.

"Say, will you marry me, my pretty maid?"
"Yes, if you please, kind sir," she said.
"What is your fortune, my pretty maid?"
"My face is my fortune, sir," she said.
"Then I can't marry you, my pretty maid!"
"Nobody asked you, sir," she said.

"NOBODY ASKED YOU, SIR," SHE SAID

From "A CHILD'S GARDEN OF VERSES"

Rain

The rain is raining all around,
  It falls on field and tree,
It rains on the umbrellas here,
  And on the ships at sea.

System

Every night my prayers I say,
And get my dinner every day;
And every day that I've been good,
I get an orange after food.

The child that is not clean and neat,
With lots of toys and things to eat,
He is a naughty child, I'm sure—
Or else his dear papa is poor.

The Cow

The friendly cow all red and white,
  I love with all my heart:
She gives me cream with all her might,
  To eat with apple-tart.

She wanders lowing here and there,
  And yet she cannot stray,
All in the pleasant open air,
  The pleasant light of day.

And blown by all the winds that pass
  And wet with all the showers,
She walks among the meadow grass
  And eats the meadow flowers.

Happy Thought

The world is so full of a number of things,
I'm sure we should all be as happy as kings.

ROBERT LOUIS STEVENSON

A KITCHEN-GARDEN OF VERSES

Rain

The rain is raining all around,
  It's raining here and there;
It washes up my lettuce seeds,
  And doesn't seem to care.

Reward

Every night my prayers I say,
And search the garden every day;
And every day, if luck is good,
I get a radish for my food.

The Cow

The friendly cow all red and white,
  I love with love intense;
She wakes me with her bell at night,
  And blunders through my fence.

She wanders like a vagrant breeze,
  Most amiable of brutes;
She tramples down my beans and peas,
  And crops the tender shoots.

Happy Thought

This world is so full of a number of bugs,
I'm sure every plant should be sprinkled with drugs.

BERT LESTON TAYLOR
(after Robert Louis Stevenson)

AT THE GARDEN GATE

Who so late
At the garden gate?
Emily, Kate,
And John.
"John,
Where have you been?
It's after six;
Supper is on,
And you've been gone
An hour,
John!"
"We've been, we've been,
We've just been over
The field," said
John.
(Emily, Kate,
And John.)

Who so late
At the garden gate?
Emily, Kate,
and John.
"John,
What
Have you got?"
"A whopping toad.

Isn't he big?
He's a terrible
Load.
(We found him
A little ways
Up the road,"
Said Emily, Kate,
And John.)

Who so late
At the garden gate?
Emily, Kate,
And John.
"John,
Put that thing down!
Do you want to get warts?"
(They all three have 'em
By last
Reports.)
Still, finding toads
Is the best of
Sports,
Say Emily,
Kate,
And John.

DAVID MC CORD

FINDING TOADS IS THE BEST OF SPORTS

ON OUR FARM

The Garden

We have a little garden
Where the biggest vegetables grow,
But how we'll ever use them all
Is something I don't know.

Yet mother eats the peas and beans,
The boys like carrots best,
While daddy dreams of corn and greens—
And Cook puts up the rest.

Our Pets

Wouldn't we have the nicest pets
If trout jumped out of the stream,
And little hens laid omelets,
And cows all gave ice-cream!

Peter and Polly

Peter is a funny cat;
His playmate is a cow.
Yet Peter can't say "Moo" like that!
And Polly can't say "Meow!"

Corn

In early spring when Samuel plows
  And then begins to sow,
I see the yellow seeds of corn,
  And wish I were a crow.

But when the corn is tall as Sam,
  And harvest time is near,
I'd rather be just what I am
  And eat it off the ear.

ESTHER ANTIN

EVENING AT THE FARM

Into the yard the farmer goes,
With grateful heart, at the close of day;
Harness and chain are hung away;
In the wagon-shed stand yoke and plow,
The straw's in the stack, the hay in the mow,
   The cooling dews are falling;
The friendly sheep their welcome bleat,
The pigs come grunting to his feet,
And the whinnying mare her master knows,
When into the yard the farmer goes,
   His cattle calling,
   "Co', boss! co', boss! co'! co'! co'!"
While still the cow-boy, far away,
Goes seeking those that have gone astray,—
   "Co', boss! co', boss! co'! co'!"

To supper at last the farmer goes.
The apples are pared, the paper read,
The stories are told, then all to bed.
Without, the crickets' ceaseless song
Makes shrill the silence all night long;
   The heavy dews are falling.
The household sinks to deep repose,
But still in sleep the farm-boy goes
   Singing, calling,
   "Co', boss! co', boss! co'! co'! co'!"
And oft the milkmaid, in her dreams,
Drums in the pail with the flashing streams,
   Murmuring, "So, boss! so!"

          JOHN TOWNSEND TROWBRIDGE

THE HARPERS' FARM

We always drive along until
We reach a humping little hill,

And on the other side of this
The farm should be and there it is,

Waiting for us, white and neat
In the misty summer heat.

And here we are and here we are,
Climbing quickly from the car

And asking may we ride the horse,
And Mrs. Harper says: "Of course."

And asking are there any new
Kittens, and she says: "A few."

And asking may we go and play
Hide and Seek up in the hay.

And in the corner of the loft
There *are* the kittens gray and soft,

With tongues just learning how to drink
And little ears all lined with pink.

Then Mrs. Harper calls "Yoo hoo!"
And so we run (we always do)

Out the barn and through a gate
And find some cookies on a plate,

Sugar on the top and cut
Like stars, and each one with a nut.

And there is also lemonade
In a pitcher in the shade.

And after that we always climb
On Bessie's back one at a time,

And Mrs. Harper laughs at us,
But it seems very dangerous,

Stuck so high up in the sun
Looking down at everyone.

We squeal and grab each other's clothes,
We hang on with our knees and toes

And say "Giddap," and Bessie does,
And such a gallop never was!

Then we get off her all alone,
Her tail a rope for sliding down.

And soon it's late and time to go,
So we tell Mrs. Harper so.

"Thanks for the lemonade," we say,
And wave good-by. And drive away.

DOROTHY ALDIS

BOYS AND GIRLS

BOYS AND GIRLS

You will recall some of the make-believe and play-pretend in this section. At one time or another, most of you have played just such games with yourselves as are described in "Hide and Seek," "Underneath the Clothes," "The Day of the Circus Horse," "The Land of Counterpane," "The Frost Pane" and "Seein' Things." You will also recognize, I'm sure, some of the girls and boys in this company of rhymes. Who doesn't remember Jack and Jill, and Little Miss Muffet, and Tom, Tom, the Piper's Son, and Curly-locks, and Georgey Porgey, and Little Polly Flinders, and Wee Willie Winkie.

But how many of you, I wonder, know Jim Jay who got stuck in Yesterday and never caught up with Today? And the foolish flying Robert whose umbrella carried him away and who was never seen again? And careless Harriet who played with matches? And ridiculous Rebecca who made a habit of slamming doors? And the four different Peters in "Prince Peter" and "The Three Peters"? And Stalky Jack, who is the same Jack who climbed the beanstalk but found, on his return, everything too small for him after living in a country sized for giants? And how many of you have played the modern game told of in "Chairoplane Chant"?

There are some queer poems here, too. Perhaps the two queerest are the ones on pages 115 and 116. Imagine a person dreaming everything in numbers like "The Dream of a Boy at Nine-Elms" and "The Dream of a Girl Who Lived at Seven-Oaks." A friend of mine lives in an English village quaintly called Five Ashes; I wonder if he dreams in fives. And if your name has anything to do with it, imagine the dreams of a person called Helen Twelve-trees! Each person must have his list of favorites—and I know what things I'd dream of if I were the boy at Nine-Elms or the girl at Seven-Oaks.

But suppose you were living at Thousand Islands!

BOYS AND GIRLS OF LONG AGO

Boys and girls, come out to play;
The moon doth shine as bright as day;
Leave your supper, and leave your sleep,
And come with your playfellows into the street.
Come with a whoop, come with a call,
Come with a good will or not at all.
Up the ladder and down the wall,
A halfpenny roll will serve us all.
You find milk and I'll find flour,
And we'll have a pudding in half an hour.

Jack and Jill
Went up the hill
To fetch a pail of water;
Jack fell down
And broke his crown,
And Jill came tumbling after.

Up he got,
And home did trot
As fast as he could caper;
Went to bed,
And wrapped his head
In vinegar and brown paper.

As Tommy Snooks and Bessie Brooks
Were walking out one Sunday,
Says Tommy Snooks to Bessie Brooks,
"Tomorrow will be Monday."

Hannah Bantry
In the pantry
Ate a mutton bone;

How she gnawed it,
How she clawed it,
When she was alone!

"Willie Boy, Willie Boy, where are you going?
I'll go with you, if I may."
"I'm going to the meadow to see them a-mowing,
And help them make the hay."

Little Miss Muffet
Sat on a tuffet,
Eating her curds and whey;
Along came a spider,
And sat down beside her,
And frightened Miss Muffet away.

Tom, Tom, the piper's son,
Stole a pig, and away he run.
The pig was eat, and Tom was beat,
And Tom went roaring down the street.

"We are three brethren out of Spain,
Come to court your daughter Jane."

"My daughter Jane she is too young,
She has not learned her mother-tongue;
But be she young, or be she old,
It's for her gold she must be sold."

"Then fare you well, my lady gay,
We'll call again another day."

When I was a little boy
I had but little wit,
'Tis a long time ago,
And I have no more yet;
Nor ever, ever shall,
Until that I die,
For the longer I live,
The more fool am I.

"Come, let's to bed,"
Says Sleepy-head;
"Tarry a while," says Slow.
"Put on the pot,"
Says Greedy-gut,
"Let's sup before we go."

Georgey Porgey,
Pudding and pie,
Kissed the girls
And made them cry;
When the girls
Came out to play,
Georgey Porgey
Ran away.

Bessie Bell and Mary Gray,
    They were two bonny lasses;
They built their house upon the lea,
    And covered it with rashes.

Bessie kept the garden gate,
    And Mary kept the pantry;
Bessie always had to wait,
    While Mary lived in plenty.

Curly-locks! Curly-locks! Wilt thou be mine?
Thou shalt not wash dishes, nor yet feed the swine,
But sit on a cushion and sew a fine seam,
And feast upon strawberries, sugar, and cream.

Little Polly Flinders
Sat among the cinders,
Warming her pretty little toes.
Her mother came and caught her,
And whipped her little daughter
For spoiling her nice new clothes.

Peter White
Will ne'er go right.
Would you know the reason why?
He follows his nose
Wherever he goes,
And there stands all awry.

Wee Willie Winkie runs through the town,
Up stairs and down stairs in his night gown;
Rapping at the window, crying through the lock,
"Are the children in bed, for it's now eight o'clock?"

What are little boys made of, made of;
What are little boys made of?
"Snips and snails, and puppy-dogs' tails;
That's what little boys are made of, made of."

What are little girls made of, made of;
What are little girls made of?
"Sugar and spice, and everything nice;
That's what little girls are made of, made of."

A dillar, a dollar,
A ten-o'clock scholar,
What makes you come so soon?
You used to come at ten o'clock,
But now you come at noon.

There was a little boy and a little girl
    Lived in an alley;
Says the little boy to the little girl,
    "Shall I, oh! shall I?"

Says the little girl to the little boy,
    "What shall we do?"
Says the little boy to the little girl,
    "I will kiss you."

There was a little girl and she had a little curl,
    Right in the middle of her forehead;
And when she was good, she was very, very good,
    But when she was bad, she was horrid!

TIT FOR TAT

Two little boys with frowsy head—
    One with gray eyes and one with blue—
Said to their mother, when tucked in bed,
    "You're so good to us 'cause we're good to you."

"We get up in the morning without any noise;
    We undress ourselves without any fuss;
You're lucky to have such good little boys;
    We're *so* good to you—so you're good to us!"

ESTHER ANTIN

MY SHADOW

I have a little shadow that goes in and out with me,
And what can be the use of him is more than I can see.
He is very, very like me from the heels up to the head;
And I see him jump before me, when I jump into my bed.

The funniest thing about him is the way he likes to grow—
Not at all like proper children, which is always very slow;
For he sometimes shoots up taller like an india-rubber ball,
And he sometimes gets so little that there's none of him at all.

He hasn't got a notion of how children ought to play,
And can only make a fool of me in every sort of way.
He stays so close beside me, he's a coward you can see;
I'd think shame to stick to Nursie as that shadow sticks to me!

One morning, very early, before the sun was up,
I rose and found the shining dew on every buttercup;
But my lazy little shadow, like an arrant sleepy-head
Had stayed at home behind me and was fast asleep in bed.

ROBERT LOUIS STEVENSON

THE LAND OF COUNTERPANE

When I was sick and lay a-bed,
I had two pillows at my head,
And all my toys beside me lay
To keep me happy all the day.

And sometimes for an hour or so
I watched my leaden soldiers go,
With different uniforms and drills,
Among the bed-clothes, through the hills;

And sometimes sent my ships in fleets
All up and down among the sheets;
Or brought my trees and houses out,
And planted cities all about.

I was the giant great and still
That sits upon the pillow-hill,
And sees before him, dale and plain,
The pleasant land of counterpane.

ROBERT LOUIS STEVENSON

FOREIGN CHILDREN

Little Indian, Sioux, or Crow,
Little frosty Eskimo,
Little Turk or Japanee—
Oh! don't you wish that you were me?

You have seen the scarlet trees,
And the lions overseas;
You have eaten ostrich eggs,
And turned the turtle off their legs.

Such a life is very fine,
But it's not as nice as mine;
You must often, as you trod,
Have wearied not to be abroad.

You have curious things to eat,
I am fed on proper meat;
You must dwell beyond the foam,
But I am safe and live at home.

Little Indian, Sioux, or Crow,
Little frosty Eskimo,
Little Turk or Japanee—
Oh! don't you wish that you were me?

ROBERT LOUIS STEVENSON

IF NO ONE EVER MARRIES ME

If no one ever marries me—
And I don't see why they should,
For Nurse says I'm not pretty,
And I'm seldom very good—

If no one ever marries me
I shan't mind very much;
I shall buy a squirrel in a cage,
And a little rabbit-hutch.

I shall have a cottage near a wood,
And a pony all my own,
And a little lamb quite clean and tame
That I can take to town.

And when I'm getting *really* old—
At twenty-eight or nine—
I shall buy a little orphan girl,
And bring her up as mine.

(If no one ever marries me—
And I don't see why they should!)

LAURENCE ALMA TADEMA

SEEIN' THINGS

I ain't afeard uv snakes, or toads, or bugs, or worms, or mice,
An' things 'at girls are skeered uv *I* think are awful nice!
I'm pretty brave, I guess; an' yet I hate to go to bed,
For, when I'm tucked up warm an' snug an' when my prayers are said,
Mother tells me "Happy dreams!" and takes away the light,
An' leaves me lyin' all alone an' seein' things at night!

Sometimes they're in the corner, sometimes they're by the door,
Sometimes they're all a-standin' in the middle uv the floor;
Sometimes they are a-sittin' down, sometimes they're walkin' round
So softly an' so creepylike they never make a sound!
Sometimes they are as black as ink, an' other times they're white—
But the color ain't no difference when you see things at night!

Once, when I licked a feller 'at had just moved on our street,
An' father sent me up to bed without a bite to eat,
I woke up in the dark an' saw things standin' in a row,
A-lookin' at me cross-eyed an' p'intin' at me—so!
Oh, my! I wuz so skeered that time I never slep' a mite—
It's almost alluz when I'm bad I see things at night!

Lucky thing I ain't a girl, or I'd be skeered to death!
Bein' I'm a boy, I duck my head an' hold my breath;
An' I am, oh! *so* sorry I'm a naughty boy, an' then
I promise to be better an' I say my prayers again!
Gran'ma tells me that's the only way to make it right
When a feller has been wicked an' sees things at night!

An' so, when other naughty boys would coax me into sin,
I try to skwush the Tempter's voice 'at urges me within;
An' when they's pie for supper, or cakes 'at's big an' nice,
I want to—but I do not pass my plate f'r them things twice!
No, ruther let Starvation wipe me slowly out of sight
Than I should keep a-livin' on an' seein' things at night!

EUGENE FIELD

DIMPLE DIGGERS

When I was very young
I said to my father,
I said to my mother,
"Mother and father," said I,
"Of lip and of ear and of tongue,
I know the what and the why;
Of tooth and of nose and of hair,
I know the when and the where—
But, father and mother,
Mother and father,
Father and mother," cried I,
"The dimple, the dimple!
Whence came the dimple?" cried I.

"The dimple?" said my father.
"The dimple?" said my mother.
"The answer," said my father.
"Is simple," said my mother.
"Is simple," said the two.

"I kissed you," said my father.
"I kissed you," said my mother.
"Kissed you," said my father.
"Kissed you," said my mother.
"And kissed you," said the two.

"Until," said the two.
"We dug," said the two.
"A dimple," said my mother.
"A dimple," said my father.
"Quite simple!" said the two.

ROBIN CHRISTOPHER

HIDE AND SEEK

When I am alone, and quite alone,
I play a game, and it's all my own.

I hide myself
Behind myself,
And then I try
To find myself.

I hide in the closet,
Where no one can see;
Then I start looking
Around for me.

I hide myself
And look for myself;
There once was a shadow
I took for myself.

I hide in a corner;
I hide in the bed;
And when I come near me
I pull in my head!

ROBIN CHRISTOPHER

HIDING

I'm hiding, I'm hiding,
And no one knows where;
For all they can see is my
Toes and my hair.

And I just heard my father
Say to my mother—
"But, darling, he must be
Somewhere or other.

"Have you looked in the inkwell?"
And mother said, "Where?"
"In the *inkwell*," said father. But
I was not there.

Then "Wait!" cried my mother—
"I think that I see
Him under the carpet." But
It was not me.

"Inside the mirror's
A pretty good place,"
Said father and looked, but saw
Only his face.

"We've hunted," sighed mother,
"As hard as we could
And I *am* so afraid that we've
Lost him for good."

Then I laughed out aloud
And I wiggled my toes
And father said—"Look, dear,
I wonder if those

"Toes could be Benny's.
There are ten of them. See?"
And they *were* so surprised to find
Out it was me!

DOROTHY ALDIS

UNDERNEATH THE CLOTHES

I'm sure that no one ever knows
The fun I have beneath the clo'es.
I snuggle down inside the bed
And cover all my face and head.

It's p'r'aps a coal-mine, p'r'aps a cave,
And sometimes, when I'm very brave,
It's Daniel's den with three or four
Or even six real lions that roar.

It's most exciting how it goes,
The road that leads beneath the clo'es;
You never *can* tell how it ends,
Because you see—it all depends.

M. NIGHTINGALE

THE DAY OF THE CIRCUS HORSE

It was a fiery circus horse
  That ramped and stamped and neighed
Till every creature in its course
  Fled, frightened and dismayed.

105

The chickens on the roadway's edge
   Arose and flapped their wings,
And making for the sheltering hedge
   Flew off like crazy things.

But when, at dusk, a little lame,
   It slowly climbed the stairs,
Behold! a gentle lady came
   And made it say its prayers.
Now, what a wondrous change you see!
   'Sh! Come and take a peep—
Here lies, as tame as tame can be,
   A little boy, asleep!

T. A. DALY

NINETY-NINE

Ninety-nine years old!
   How many candles does that make
   On a birthday cake?

And when I went to school
   My head would reach up to the ceiling;
   A funny feeling.

Why am I only four?
   All children want to be ninety-nine
   Or more.

CAROLYN HANCOCK

STARS

Little stars have five sharp wings,
   And they fly
   Up in the sky.

Little stars see funny things,
    Like a boat
    In the dark afloat.

And other stars in golden rings
    Slashing round
    The boat and round.

Little stars have five sharp wings.
        CAROLYN HANCOCK

TIME TO RISE

A birdie with a yellow bill
Hopped upon the window sill,
Cocked his shining eye and said:
"Ain't you 'shamed, you sleepy-head!"
        ROBERT LOUIS STEVENSON

STOUT

Alas, I am a heavy child,
    A very heavy one;
I cannot do the fearful things
    That other boys have done.

I try to caper on the green,
    I try to skip and run,
But all my buttons they burst off
    And make my clothes undone.

It is a very sad, sad thing
    To be so fat a child,
To have to merely sit about,
    And yet to feel quite wild.
        RUE CARPENTER

THE LIAR

I've done a very frightful thing,
    A thing too bad to tell:
I've told a horrid, horrid lie,
    And now I don't feel well.

I took a pastry from a shelf,
    I ate it all alone;
I never noticed how it went
    Until it was quite gone.

And when my mother she came in
    And asked me did I eat it,
I answered "No" quite loud and clear
    And then I did repeat it.

And now I have come far out here,
    My body bent with pain;
That lie it stands and glares at me
    With all its might and main!

RUE CARPENTER

THE FROST PANE

What's the good of breathing
On the window
Pane
In summer?
You can't make a frost
On the window pane
In summer.

You can't write a
Nalphabet,
You can't draw a
Nelephant;
You can't make a smudge
With your nose
(In summer).

Lots of good, breathing
On the window
Pane
In winter.
You can make a frost
On the window pane
In winter.
A white frost, a light frost,
A thick frost, a quick frost,
A write-me-out-a-picture frost
Across
The pane
In
Winter.

DAVID MC CORD

WALTZING MICE

Every night as I go to bed
I think of the prayer I should have said;
And even now as I bow my head:
"Please, O Lord, may I have instead
Some waltzing mice, a gun, and a sled?"

I don't suppose they're much of a price,
But Uncle Ted (without advice)
Gave me skates, and there isn't ice;
And I could have been saying, "How terribly *nice,*
A gun, a sled, and waltzing mice!"

Every night when play is done,
I think them all over, one by one;
"And quite the splendidest, Lord, for fun
Are waltzing mice, a sled, and a gun."

DAVID MC CORD

EMILY JANE

Oh! Christmas time is coming again,
And what shall I buy for Emily Jane?
O Emily Jane, my love so true,
Now what upon earth shall I buy for you?
My Emily Jane, my doll so dear,
I've loved you now for many a year,
And still while there's anything left of you,
My Emily Jane, I'll love you true!

My Emily Jane has lost her head,
And has a potato tied on instead;
A hole for an eye, and a lump for a nose,
It really looks better than you would suppose.
My Emily Jane has lost her arms,
The half of one leg's the extent of her charms;
But still, while there's anything left of you,
My Emily Jane, I'll love you true.

And now, shall I bring you a fine new head,
Or shall I bring you a leg instead?
Or will you have arms, to hug me tight,
When naughty 'Lizabeth calls you a fright?

Or I'll buy you a dress of satin so fine,
'Mong all the dolls to shimmer and shine;
For oh! while there's anything left of you,
My Emily Jane, I'll love you true!

Mamma says, "Keep all your pennies, Sue,
And I'll buy you a doll all whole and new."
But better I love my dear old doll,
With her one half-leg and potato poll.
"The potato may rot, and the leg may fall?"
Well, then I shall treasure the sawdust, that's all!
For while there is *anything* left of you,
My Emily Jane, I'll love you true!

LAURA E. RICHARDS

KATE

Kate was a pretty child
Five years old;
But her hair wouldn't brush
Because it was gold.
Her eyes wouldn't shut
Because they were flowers,
Yet she could weep
Like April showers.
Kate was a nice child
Four feet high;
She could run like the wind,
Though not in the sky;
But her throat was of marble
So she couldn't speak;
And some people think
That Kate was a freak.

HELEN UNDERWOOD HOYT

JONATHAN BING

Poor old Jonathan Bing
Went out in his carriage to visit the King,
But everyone pointed and said, "Look at that!
Jonathan Bing has forgotten his hat!"
(He'd forgotten his hat!)

Poor old Jonathan Bing
Went home and put on a new hat for the King,
But by the palace a soldier said, "Hi!
You can't see the King; you've forgotten your tie!"
(He'd forgotten his tie!)

Poor old Jonathan Bing,
He put on a beautiful tie for the King,
But when he arrived, an Archbishop said, "Ho!
You can't come to court in pyjamas, you know!"
(He'd come in pyjamas!)

Poor old Jonathan Bing
Went home and addressed a short note to the King:
"If you please will excuse me, I won't come to tea;
For home's the best place for all people like me!"

BEATRICE CURTIS BROWN

JONATHAN BING DOES ARITHMETIC

When Jonathan Bing was young, they say,
He shirked his lessons and ran away—
Sat in a meadow and twiddled his thumbs,
And never learnt spelling or did any sums.

So now if you tell him, "Add 1 to 2."
"I don't understand!" he'll answer you,
"Do you mean 2-day or that's 2 bad?
And what sort of 1 do you want me to add?"

"For there's 1 who was first when the race was 1,
Though perhaps 2 many were trying to run;
So if 2 had 1 when the race was through,
I'd say the answer was 1 by 2!"

"O Jonathan Bing, you haven't the trick
Of doing a sum in arithmetic!"
"O give me a chance, just one more try!"
Cries Jonathan Bing with a tear in his eye.

"Very well, Jonathan, just once more.
What is a hundred plus seventy-four?"
"A hundred—and seventy-four?" says he,
"Why! That's a great age for a person to be!"

BEATRICE CURTIS BROWN

STALKY JACK

I knew a boy who took long walks,
Who lived on beans and ate the stalks;
To the Giants' Country he lost his way;
They kept him there for a year and a day.
But he has not been the same boy since;
An alteration he did evince;
For you may suppose that he underwent
A change in his notions of extent!

He looks with contempt on a nice high door,
And tries to walk in at the second floor;
He stares with surprise at a basin of soup,
He fancies a bowl as large as a hoop;
He calls the people "minikin mites";
He calls a sirloin a couple of bites!
Things having come to these pretty passes,
They bought him some magnifying glasses.

He put on the goggles, and said, "My eyes!
The world has come to its proper size!"
But all the boys cry, "Stalky John!
There you go with your goggles on!"
What girl would marry him—and quite right—
To be taken for three times her proper height?
So this comes of taking extravagant walks,
And living on beans, and eating the stalks.

WILLIAM BRIGHTY RANDS

THE DREAM OF A BOY AT NINE-ELMS

Nine grenadiers, with bayonets in their guns;
Nine bakers' baskets, with hot-cross buns;
Nine brown elephants, standing in a row;
Nine new velocipedes, good ones to go;
Nine knickerbocker suits, with buttons all complete;
Nine pair of skates with straps for the feet;
Nine clever conjurers eating hot coals;
Nine sturdy mountaineers leaping on their poles;
Nine little drummer-boys beating on their drums;
Nine fat aldermen sitting on their thumbs;
Nine new knockers to our front door;
Nine new neighbors that I never saw before;
Nine times running I dreamt it all plain;
With bread and cheese for supper I could dream it all again!

WILLIAM BRIGHTY RANDS

THE DREAM OF A GIRL WHO LIVED AT SEVEN-OAKS

Seven sweet singing birds up in a tree;
Seven swift sailing-ships white upon the sea;
Seven bright weather-cocks shining in the sun;
Seven slim race-horses ready for a run;
Seven gold butterflies, flitting overhead;
Seven red roses blowing in a garden bed;
Seven white lilies, with honey bees inside them;
Seven round rainbows with clouds to divide them;
Seven pretty little girls with sugar on their lips;

Seven witty little boys, whom everybody tips;
Seven nice fathers, to call little maids joys;
Seven nice mothers, to kiss the little boys;
Seven nights running I dreamt it all plain;
With bread and jam for supper I could dream it all again!

WILLIAM BRIGHTY RANDS

A BOY'S SONG

Where the pools are bright and deep,
Where the gray trout lies asleep,
Up the river and over the lea,
That's the way for Billy and me.

Where the blackbird sings the latest,
Where the hawthorn blooms the sweetest,
Where the nestlings chirp and flee,
That's the way for Billy and me.

Where the mowers mow the cleanest,
Where the hay lies thick and greenest,
There to track the homeward bee,
That's the way for Billy and me.

Where the hazel bank is steepest,
Where the shadow falls the deepest,
Where the clustering nuts fall free,
That's the way for Billy and me.

This I know, I love to play
Through the meadow, among the hay;
Up the water and over the lea,
That's the way for Billy and me.

JAMES HOGG

CHAIROPLANE CHANT

If everyone had a flying machine
The size of a small armchair,
Then day after day, in the promptest way
I'd go out to take the air.
I'd shift a lever and press a brake,
And buzz into the blue.
Oho, the bushels of air I'd take,
Flying to call on you.

As I skirted a steeple and skimmed a roof,
With engine whirring loud,
I'd meet you coming for dear life, humming
Around the rim of a cloud.
We'd dodge a swallow and duck a crow,
And you would cry, "Whoopee!
I was going to call on you, you know—
Were you coming to call on me?"

It's rather awkward to chat, of course,
From a high-geared chairoplane,
So we'd buzz away. But the very next day
We'd meet in a sky-blue lane,
With wind in our wings, and the way all clear,
And I'd sing, "Ho, halloo,
Were you coming to call on me? *O dear,*
I was going to call on you!"

                                        NANCY BYRD TURNER

117

PRINCE PETER

Young Prince Peter suddenly, once,
For no real reason behaved like a dunce.

His bath was ready that summer morning,
But he said very loud (without any warning):

"Who wants to scrub—oh, pish, oh, stuff!—
In a silly old tub? I am clean enough!"

He threw out the towels, and soap, and then—
"I never," he cried, "will bathe again!"

And rushed to the garden, wild and foolish,
Kicking his heels and being mulish.

All of the pansies were in their places,
The sun just drying their new-washed faces.

A toad went skittering down the path,
Bound for a puddle, to take a bath.

A robin dipped in a clear, brown pool;
He thought Prince Peter was rather a fool.

"Hist!" he said to a startled wren,
"The Prince is never to bathe again."

Down by the duck-pond Diddles and Daddles
Pushed through the water with legs like paddles.

They dived and chuckled, "He'll bathe no more."
Puss sat stiff by the kitchen door,

Washing her children, five fat kittens,
With pearl-white collars and pearl-gray mittens.

She washed each kitten from toe to crown,
And cuffed it lightly to polish it down.

They sang with happiness in their throats—
Stiff-starched whiskers and shiny coats.

They gazed at Peter, who stood abashed,
They mourned, "He'll never again be washed."

All at once, with a drooping head,
Into the palace Peter fled.

His buttons were popping as he flew;
He flung off his collar and kicked off his shoe;

Into the bathroom wildly burst,
Into the bathtub hopped head first.

"Hurrp and humph!" he said, with a splash,
" 'Twould be so lonesome never to wash!"

And from that time on there was never a neater
Boy in the kingdom than young Prince Peter.

NANCY BYRD TURNER

THE PICNIC

They had a picnic in the woods,
And Mother couldn't go that day,
But the twins and Brother and I could go;
We rode on the wagon full of hay.

There were more little girls than ten, I guess.
And the boy that is Joe B. Kirk was there.
He found a toad and a katydid,
And a little girl came whose name was Clare.

Miss Kate-Marie made us play a song
Called "Fare-you-well, says Johnny O'Brown."
You dance in a ring and sing it through,
And then someone kneels down.

She kissed us all and Joe B. Kirk;
But Joe B. didn't mind a bit.
He walked around and swung his arms
And seemed to be very glad of it.

Then Mr. Jim said he would play,
But Miss Marie, she told him then,
It's a game for her and the little folks,
And he could go and fish with the men.

Mr. Wells was there and he had a rope
To tie to a limb and make it swing.
And Mrs. Wells, Mr. Wells' wife,
Gave me a peach and a chicken wing.

And I had a little cherry pie
And a piece of bread, and after we'd played
Two other songs, I had some cake,
And another wing and some lemonade.

ELIZABETH MADOX ROBERTS

THE PERFECT CHILD

I am without a single doubt
　　The world's most perfect child.
I never cry, or play, or shout;
　　It's vulgar to be wild.
To games which seem to everyone
The very finest sort of fun,
I say, "No, thanks; I never run.
　　It isn't done."

An outdoor picnic gives me fits—
  Always a fence to climb!
An indoor party bores me, it's
  A silly waste of time.
And as for any kind of "spread,"
Ice cream or cake, when all is said
I'd much prefer to have instead
  A crust of bread.

I cannot bear the sight of toys—
  So take them all away.
I have so many other joys
  To fill my busy day!
Arithmetic's my greatest glee;
I love the dates in History;
And best of all the sports to me:
  Geography.

Sometimes my uncle sends his car
  To take me to the plays;
But I refuse, for theaters are
  So stupid nowadays.
My teachers say my place is high
Among the angels in the sky . . .
What! Do you think my teachers lie?
  Well, so do I.

MOLLY MICHAELS

THE THREE PETERS

The first was a gray-beard Peter,
    And a very wise man was he.
Whatever the shock, he stood like a rock,
    And he carried a great, gold Key.
He once was as poor as a fisher
    On the waters of Galilee;
But his life had no taint, and now he's a saint—
    All that a Peter should be.

Came Peter the Terrible Eater,
    Who pounced on each morsel with glee;
Pickled peppers he'd pick by the peck, and grew sick
    When he found that they wouldn't agree.
Alas, for this poor Peter Piper,
    His end was a horrible spree:
He minded his "q's" but he couldn't refuse
    Anything that began with a "P"!

The last was a puck of a Peter
   Who lived in the twigs of a tree;
Part fairy, part friend, he taught little white Wendy
   To fly, and how happy was she.
The Indians loved him, and Pirates
   Soon learned who was King of the Sea.
Though his mother might scold, he would never grow old–
   And that is the Peter for me,
        Oh, yes,
  Oh, Pan is the Peter for me!

                    MOLLY MICHAELS

123

THE YOUNG THING

"Where have you been all the day,
  My boy Willy?"
"I've been all the day
Courting of a lady gay:
But, oh! she's too young
To be taken from her mammy."

"What work can she do,
  My boy Willy?
Can she bake and can she brew,
  My boy Willy?"
"She can brew and she can bake,
And she can make our wedding-cake:
But, oh! she's too young
To be taken from her mammy."

"What age may she be? What age may she be?
  My boy Willy?"
"Twice two, twice seven,
Twice ten, twice eleven:
But, oh! she's too young
To be taken from her mammy."

OLD SONG

TO MY SON

Aged three years and five months

Thou happy, happy elf!
(But stop,—first let me kiss away that tear)—
Thou tiny image of myself!
(My love, he's poking peas into his ear!)
Thou merry laughing sprite!
With spirits feather-light,
Untouched by sorrow, and unsoiled by sin—
(Good heavens! the child is swallowing a pin!)
Thou little tricky Puck!
With antic toys so funnily bestuck,
Light as the singing bird that wings the air—
(The door! the door! He'll tumble down the stair!)
Thou darling of thy sire!
(Why, Janet, he'll set his pinafore a-fire!)
Thou imp of mirth and joy!
In love's dear chain so strong and bright a link,
Thou idol of thy parents—(Drat the boy!
There goes my ink!)

THOMAS HOOD

HIAWATHA'S CHILDHOOD

There the wrinkled, old Nokomis
Nursed the little Hiawatha,
Rocked him in his linden cradle,
Bedded soft in moss and rushes,
Safely bound with reindeer sinews;
Stilled his fretful wail by saying,
"Hush! the Naked Bear will get thee!"
Lulled him into Slumber, singing,
"Ewa-yea! my little owlet!
Who is this, that lights the wigwam?
With his great eyes lights the wigwam?
Ewa-yea! my little owlet!"

Many things Nokomis taught him
Of the stars that shine in heaven;
Showed him Ishkoodah, the comet,
Ishkoodah, with fiery tresses;
Showed the Death-Dance of the spirits,
Warriors with their plumes and war-clubs,
Flaring far away to northward
In the frosty nights of Winter;
Showed the broad, white road in heaven,
Pathway of the ghosts, the shadows,
Running straight across the heavens,
Crowded with the ghosts, the shadows.

At the door on summer evenings
Sat the little Hiawatha;
Heard the whispering of the pine-trees,
Heard the lapping of the water,
Sounds of music, words of wonder;
"Minne-wawa!" said the pine-trees,
"Mudway-aushka!" said the water.

Saw the fire-fly, Wah-wah-taysee,
Flitting through the dusk of evening,
With the twinkle of its candle
Lighting up the brakes and bushes,
And he sang the song of children,
Sang the song Nokomis taught him:
"Wah-wah-taysee, little fire-fly,
Little, flitting, white-fire insect,
Little, dancing, white-fire creature,
Light me with your little candle,
Ere upon my bed I lay me,
Ere in sleep I close my eyelids!"

Saw the moon rise from the water,
Rippling, rounding from the water,
Saw the flecks and shadows on it,
Whispered, "What is that, Nokomis?"
And the good Nokomis answered:
"Once a warrior, very angry,
Seized his grandmother, and threw her
Up into the sky at midnight;
Right against the moon he threw her;
'Tis her body that you see there."

Saw the rainbow in the heaven,
In the eastern sky, the rainbow,
Whispered, "What is that, Nokomis?"
And the good Nokomis answered:
" 'Tis the heaven of flowers you see there;
All the wild-flowers of the forest,
All the lilies of the prairie,
When on earth they fade and perish,
Blossom in that heaven above us."

When he heard the owls at midnight,
Hooting, laughing in the forest,
"What is that?" he cried in terror;
"What is that?" he said, "Nokomis?"
And the good Nokomis answered:
"That is but the owl and owlet,
Talking in their native language,
Talking, scolding at each other."

Then the little Hiawatha
Learned of every bird its language,
Learned their names and all their secrets,
How they built their nests in Summer,
Where they hid themselves in Winter,
Talked with them whene'er he met them,
Called them "Hiawatha's Chickens."

Of all beasts he learned the language,
Learned their names and all their secrets,
How the beavers built their lodges,
Where the squirrels hid their acorns,
How the reindeer ran so swiftly,
Why the rabbit was so timid;
Talked with them whene'er he met them,
Called them "Hiawatha's Brothers."

HENRY WADSWORTH LONGFELLOW

CHILDHOOD

I could know
    Wonders wild
If I could grow
    Up to a child.

It is no myth
    That a child can unfence
Paradise with
    Its innocence.

An eager child
    Will breathlessly push
Through jungles wild
    In a backyard bush.

It will begin
    Exploring for new
Edens in
    Each drop of dew.

A man has not
    Child's gift for this
Being what
    It really is.

A child leaps free
    From what it seems:
A child can be
    The thing it dreams.

LOUIS GINSBERG

129

UNDERNEATH HIS RED UMBRELLA

THE STORY OF FLYING ROBERT

When the rain comes tumbling down
In the country or the town,
All good little girls and boys
Stay at home and mind their toys.
Robert thought, "No, when it pours,
It is better out of doors."
Rain it *did,* and in a minute
Bob was in it.
Here you see him, silly fellow,
Underneath his red umbrella.

What a wind! Oh! how it whistles
Through the trees and flowers and thistles!
It has caught his red umbrella;
Now look at him, silly fellow,
Up he flies
To the skies.
No one heard his screams and cries,
Through the clouds the rude wind bore him,
And his hat flew on before him.
Soon they got to such a height,
They were nearly out of sight!
And the hat went up so high,
That it really touched the sky.

Rainbow in the Sky

No one ever yet could tell
Where they stopped or where they fell:
Only, this one thing is plain,
Bob was never seen again!

From the German of Heinrich Hoffmann

HARRIET AND THE MATCHES

It's really almost past belief
How little Harriet came to grief.
Mamma and Nurse went out one day
And left her all alone to play;
Now, on the table close at hand,
A box of matches chanced to stand;
And kind Mamma and Nurse had told her,
That, if she touched them, they should scold her.
But Harriet said: "Oh, what a pity!
For, when they burn, it is *so* pretty;
They snap, and burn from red to blue;
All other people light them, too."

    The pussy-cats heard this,
    And they began to hiss,
    And stretch their claws
    And raise their paws;
    "Me-ow," they said, "me-ow, me-o!
    You'll burn to death if you do so."

But Harriet would not take advice,
She lit a match, it was so nice!
It crackled so, it burned so clear,—
Exactly like the picture here.
She jumped for joy and ran about
And was too pleased to put it out.

The pussy-cats saw this
And said: "Oh, naughty, naughty Miss!"
And stretched their claws
And raised their paws:
" 'Tis very, very wrong, you know,
Me-ow, mee-o, me-ow, me-o!
You will be burnt, if you do so."

And see! Oh! what a dreadful thing!
The fire has caught an apron-string;
Her apron burns, her arms, her hair;
She burns all over, everywhere.

Then how the pussy-cats did mew,
What else, poor pussies, could they do?
They screamed for help, 'twas all in vain!
So then they said: "We'll scream again;
Make haste, make haste, me-ow, me-o.
She'll burn to death, we told her so."

So she was burnt, with all her clothes,
And arms, and hands, and eyes and nose;
Till she had nothing more to lose
Except her little scarlet shoes . . .
And nothing else but these was found
Among her ashes on the ground.

From the German of Heinrich Hoffmann

135

REBECCA

Who slammed Doors for Fun and Perished Miserably

A Trick that everyone abhors
In Little Girls is slamming Doors.
A Wealthy Banker's little Daughter
Who lived in Palace Green, Bayswater
(By name Rebecca Offendort),
Was given to this Furious Sport.
She would deliberately go
And Slam the door like Billy-Ho!
To make her Uncle Jacob start.
She was not really bad at heart,
But only rather rude and wild;
She was an Aggravating Child.

It happened that a Marble Bust
Of Abraham was standing just
Above the Door this little Lamb
Had carefully prepared to Slam,
And down it came! It knocked her flat!
It laid her out! She looked like that!

.   .   .   .   .

Her Funeral Sermon (which was long
And followed by a Sacred Song)
Mentioned her Virtues, it is true,
But dwelt upon her Vices, too,
And showed the Dreadful End of One
Who goes and slams the Door for Fun.

HILAIRE BELLOC

GODOLPHIN HORNE

Who was cursed with the Sin of Pride, and Became a Boot-Black

Godolphin Horne was Nobly Born;
He held the Human Race in Scorn,
And lived with all his Sisters where
His Father lived, in Berkeley Square.
And oh! the Lad was Deathly Proud!
He never shook your Hand or Bowed,
But merely smirked and nodded thus:
How perfectly ridiculous!
Alas! That such Affected Tricks
Should flourish in a Child of Six!
(For such was Young Godolphin's age.)
Just then, the Court required a Page,
Whereat the Lord High Chamberlain
(The Kindest and the Best of Men),
He went good-naturedly and took
A Perfectly Enormous Book
Called "People Qualified to Be
Attendant on His Majesty,"
And murmured, as he scanned the list
(To see that no one should be missed),
"There's William Coutts has got the Flu,
And Billy Higgs would Never do,
And Guy de Vere is far too young,
And . . . wasn't D'Alton's Father hung?

137

And as for Alexander Byng—! . . .
I think I know the kind of thing,
A Churchman, cleanly, nobly born,
Come, let us say Godolphin Horne."

But hardly had he said the word
When Murmurs of Dissent were heard.
The King of Iceland's Eldest Son
Said, "Thank you! I am taking none!"
The Agéd Duchess of Athlone
Remarked, in her sub-acid tone,
"I doubt if He is what we need!"
With which the Bishops all agreed;
And even Lady Mary Flood
(*So* kind, and, oh, so *really* good)
Said, "No. He wouldn't do at all,
He'd make us feel a lot too small."

The Chamberlain said, "Well, well, well.
No doubt you're right . . . One cannot tell!"
He took his Gold and Diamond Pen
And Scratched Godolphin out again.

So now Godolphin is the Boy
Who blacks the Boots at the Savoy.

HILAIRE BELLOC

JIM JAY

Do diddle di do,
   Poor Jim Jay
Got stuck fast
   In Yesterday.
Squinting he was,
   On cross-legs bent,
Never heeding
   The wind was spent.
Round veered the weathercock,
   The sun drew in—
And stuck was Jim
   Like a rusty pin . . .
We pulled and we pulled
   From seven till twelve,
Jim, too frightened
   To help himself.

But all in vain.
   The clock struck one,
And there was Jim
   A little bit gone.
At half-past five
   You scarce could see
A glimpse of his flapping
   Handkerchee.
And when came noon,
   And we climbed sky-high,
Jim was a speck
   Slip-slipping by.
Come tomorrow,
   The neighbors say,
He'll be past crying for;
   Poor Jim Jay.

WALTER DE LA MARE

RIDDLES IN RHYME

RIDDLES IN RHYME

A riddle is something that makes us guess the answer—and often fools us. Sometimes it seems as though there can be only one answer, and a simple one; but usually there is a twist or a trick in the lines that puts us off.

You will recognize some of these riddles at once. Everyone knows the answer to "Humpty Dumpty" and "Old Mother Twitchet." But others, even some of the old ones in "Twenty-one Old Riddles," may be strange to you. You may have to think two or three times before you decide on your answer—and even then you may not be too sure.

The puzzlers by Jonathan Swift are a little harder. They were written over a hundred years ago by a man who wrote several books which have delighted people with their pointed cleverness. One of these, "Gulliver's Travels," has been read by hundreds of thousands, and enjoyed by young and old, ever since it was written.

The puzzles by Nancy Birckhead are new, and have not been printed before in any volume. The little riddle by Dorothy Aldis is almost as new. You will find other delightful verses by this writer on other pages in this book.

Before you decide on what each puzzle may mean, read it to someone else and have him (or her) try to guess the answer. Then, to make sure who is right and who is wrong, turn to page 155, at the end of this section. There you will find the correct answers.

TWENTY-ONE OLD RIDDLES

1

Little Nancy Etticoat
In a white petticoat
  And a red rose.
The longer she stands,
  The shorter she grows.

2

Old Mother Twitchet had but one eye,
And a long tail which she let fly;
And every time she went through a gap
She left a bit of her tail in a trap.

3

I have a little sister. They call her Peep-peep;
She wades the waters deep, deep, deep;
She climbs the mountains high, high, high;
Poor little creature, she has but one eye.

4

Long legs, crooked thighs,
Little head, and no eyes.

5

In marble walls as white as milk,
Lined with a skin as soft as silk;
Within a fountain crystal clear,
A golden apple doth appear.
No doors there are to this stronghold,
Yet thieves break in and steal the gold.

6

Humpty Dumpty sat on a wall;
Humpty Dumpty had a great fall;
All the king's horses and all the king's men
Couldn't put Humpty Dumpty together again.

7

Flower of England, fruit of Spain
Met together in a shower of rain;
Put in a bag tied 'round with a string—
If you'll tell me this riddle, I'll give you a ring.

8

Thomas à Tattamus took two T's
To tie two tups to two tall trees,
To frighten the terrible Thomas à Tattamus—
Tell me how many T's there are in THAT.

9

I went to the wood and got it;
I sat me down and looked at it;
The more I looked at it the less I liked it;
And I brought it home because I couldn't help it.

10

There was a girl in our town,
Silk an' satin was her gown,
Silk an' satin, gold an' velvet—
Guess her name; three times I've telled it.

11

Thirty white horses upon a red hill;
Now they tramp, now they champ,
Now they stand still.

12

Formed long ago yet made today,
  Employed while others sleep;
What few would like to give away,
  Nor any wish to keep.

13

Black we are, though much admired.
Men seek for us till they are tired.
We tire the horse, but comfort man.
Tell me this riddle if you can.

14

Elizabeth, Lizzie, Betsy, and Bess,
All went together to seek a bird's nest.
They found a bird's nest with five eggs in;
They all took one, yet left four in.

15

As I was going to St. Ives
I met a man with seven wives;
Every wife had seven sacks;
Every sack had seven cats;
Every cat had seven kits.
Kits, cats, sacks, and wives—
How many were going to St. Ives?

16

Two legs sat upon three legs,
With one leg in his lap;
In comes four legs,
And runs away with one leg.
Up jumps two legs,
Catches up three legs,
Throws it after four legs,
And makes him bring back one leg.

17

Black within,
Red without,
Four corners
Round about.

18

As I went through the garden gap,
Who should I meet but Dick Red-cap.
A stick in his hand, and a stone in his throat.
If you'll tell me this riddle, I'll give you a groat.

19

A houseful, a roomful;
You can't catch a spoonful.

20

Round as a biscuit;
Busy as a bee;
Prettiest little thing
You ever did see.

21

Rail-road crossing,
Look out for the cars.
Bet you can't spell it
Without any R's.

AN IRISH RIDDLE

From house to house he goes;
So sure and yet so slight.
And, whether it rains or snows,
He sleeps outside all night.

AS THE WORLD TURNS

I'm up and down and round about,
Yet all the world can't find me out.
Though hundreds have employed their leisure,
They never yet could take my measure.
I'm found in almost every garden,
Nay, in the compass of a farthing.
There's not a chariot, coach, nor mill,
Can move an inch except I will.

JONATHAN SWIFT

THE FIVE

We are little airy creatures,
All of different voice and features.
One of us in glass is set;
One of us you'll find in jet;
T'other you may see in tin;
And the fourth a box within;
If the fifth you should pursue,
It can never fly from you.

JONATHAN SWIFT

WHITER THAN WHITE

From Heaven I fall, though from earth I begin;
No lady alive can show such a skin.
I'm bright as an angel, and light as a feather,
But heavy and dark when you squeeze me together.

JONATHAN SWIFT

IN A GLASS

By something formed, I nothing am,
Yet everything that you can name.
In no place have I ever been,
Yet everywhere I may be seen.
In all things false, yet always true,
I'm still the same but ever new.
Lifeless, life's perfect form I wear,
Can show a nose, eye, tongue, or ear,
Yet neither smell, see, taste, or hear . . .
Like thought, I'm in a moment gone,
Nor can I ever be alone.
All things on earth I imitate
Faster than Nature can create.
A giant now, and straight an elf,
I am everyone, but ne'er myself.
I ne'er was born, nor e'er can die.
Then, pr'ythee tell me, what am I?

JONATHAN SWIFT

EVERYWHERE

I rise from the earth, I fall from on high;
I span the whole world, yet I'm held in the eye.

Far finer than mist, in a tempest I loom,
Man's greatest blessing, his fearfulest doom.

Silent I come or with hideous moan,
Too airy to hold, or turned solid as stone.

I kill many men, yet without me they die . . .
Sail through the furthermost reaches of sky
Or plunge through the bowels of earth—there am I.

NANCY BIRCKHEAD

HERE I AM

I have no strength nor substance, yet I shake
Prophet and priest, and cause great kings to quake.

Nothing can hurt me, yet I can destroy
Man's dearest dreams or make him weep with joy.

Sometimes I'm forced to sigh, sometimes to sing,
Yet I have power over everything.

Men follow me, though few may understand;
I creep, I leap, I cringe, and I command.

And, though I'm found in every foreign land,
I'm here, beneath your eyes, close to your hand.

NANCY BIRCKHEAD

CURIOUS BUT TRUE

Washington scarcely knew them
    As he went on his way;
Lincoln seldom met them
    After he had his say;
God cannot ever see them—
    Yet Man sees them every day.

              NANCY BIRCKHEAD

THE STRANGE TEETH

Forty teeth have I complete,
Yet I've never learned to eat;
Sometimes black and sometimes white,
Yet I cannot even bite!

              NANCY BIRCKHEAD

WHAT AM I?

They chose me from my brothers: "That's the
Nicest one," they said,
And they carved me out a face and put a
Candle in my head;

And they set me on the doorstep. Oh, the
Night was dark and wild;
But when they lit the candle, then I
Smiled!

              DOROTHY ALDIS

153

MY WHAT-IS-IT

He has dust in his eye, a fan for a wing,
An elegant leg with which he can sing,
And a mouth full of dye-stuff instead of a sting.

ROBERT FROST

A LETTER FOR YOU

'Twas whispered in Heaven, 'twas muttered in Hell,
And echo caught faintly the sound as it fell;
On the confines of earth 'twas permitted to rest,
And the depths of the ocean its presence confessed.
'Twill be found in the sphere when 'tis riven asunder,
Be seen in the lightning and heard in the thunder;
'Twas allotted to man with his earliest breath,
Attends him at birth and awaits him in death,
Presides o'er his happiness, honor, and health,
Is the prop of his house and the end of his wealth.
In the heaps of the miser 'tis hoarded with care,
But is sure to be lost on his prodigal heir . . .
'Twill soften the heart; but, though deaf to the ear,
'Twill make it acutely and instantly hear.
Set in shade, let it rest like a delicate flower;
Ah! breathe on it softly, it dies in an hour.

CATHERINE FANSHAWE

ANSWERS TO "RIDDLES IN RHYME"

"Twenty-one Old Riddles."

1, on page 145: *A candle.*

2, on page 145: *A needle and thread.*

3, on page 145: *A star.*

4, on page 145: *A pair of tongs.*

5, on page 146: *An egg.*

6, on page 146: *Also an egg.*

7, on page 146: *A plum-pudding.* (Plum-puddings used to be put in a cheese-cloth bag before being boiled. They still are.)

8, on page 146: *Two.* (There are only two t's in the word "that.")

9, on page 146: *A thorn.*

10, on page 147: *Ann.*

11, on page 147: *Teeth and gums.*

12, on page 147: *A bed.*

13, on page 147: *Coals.*

14, on page 147: *"They" left four in, because "they" are all one person; Lizzie, Betsy, and Bess being nicknames for Elizabeth.*

15, on page 148: *One.* (The wives, sacks, cats, and kits have nothing to do with his going to St. Ives.)

16, on page 148: *A man* (two legs); *a stool* (three legs); *a leg of mutton* (one leg); *a dog* (four legs).

17, on page 148: *A chimney.*

18, on page 148: *A cherry.*

19, on page 149: *Smoke.*

20, on page 149: *A watch.*

21, on page 149: *Of course you can spell it without any R's, for there isn't an r in "it."*

"An Irish Riddle," on page 149: *A country lane.*
"As the World Turns," on page 150: *A Circle.*
"The Five," on page 150: *The vowels, a, e, i, o, u.*
"Whiter than White," on page 151: *Snow.*
"In a Glass," on page 151: *A shadow, or a reflection in a mirror.*
"Everywhere," on page 152: *Water.*
"Here I Am," on page 152: *The printed word.*
"Curious but True," on page 153: *His equals.*
"The Strange Teeth," on page 153: *A comb.*
"What Am I?" on page 153: *A Hallowe'en Pumpkin.*
"My What-is-it," on page 154: *A Grasshopper.*
"A Letter for You," on page 154: *The letter H.*

Winds, Weathers, Seasons, Charms

WINDS, WEATHERS, SEASONS, CHARMS

Here are poems about all sorts of winds, about fair weather and stormy weather, about the months, seasons, and changes of the year. You wouldn't think, would you, that so many different kinds of poems could be written just about the wind. Yet here are the old country "signs" by which the farmers have always said they could tell what kind of weather the wind was bringing. And here are many newer poems: Christina Rossetti's lovely and simple "The Wind," and W. H. Davies' even simpler "Happy Wind," and Robert Louis Stevenson's galloping "Windy Nights," and Robert Frost's early spring welcome "To the Thawing Wind."

Most of us prefer clear weather and sunny hours, and, offhand, a rainy day doesn't seem a pretty subject for poetry. Yet poets don't always write about pretty things, and many beautiful lines have been written about cloudy days, and rain, and storm. Read Shelley's "The Cloud"—the original poem is three times as long—and see how a great imagination finds the beauty, as well as the blessings, of cloudiness. Look at the charming way Robin Christopher treats these things in "The Storm." As for rain—the old poem by E. Jenner ("Signs of Rain") lists a lot of sayings and superstitions which are still believed today in many places. Robin Christopher, in "Rain," tells what a child thinks the rain means. W. H. Davies shows the rain's goodness. Robert Loveman's "April Rain" sees the flowers springing up, actually born in every drop, and a popular song has been built around the fanciful idea. Longfellow's "Rain in Summer"—the two verses in this group are part of a much longer poem—gives the look and the sound and the very feel of a downpour "clattering along the roofs, like the tramp of hoofs" after a spell of heat.

Wordsworth's "Written in March" is something of a rain-poem, but it shows what happens *after* the rain, and is one of the clearest pictures in all poetry. Poems about the budding season are countless, but there never has been a livelier one than Thomas Nashe's and a merrier or more innocent one than William Blake's "Spring."

The verses in "Signs and Seasons" collect sayings about rain, winds, bees, and seasons that are heard in different parts of England and America. The "Charms" are almost as common. I have heard grown people catch their breath at the sight of a hay-wagon and repeat:

> Load of hay!
> Load of hay!
> Make a wish
> And turn away!

I don't know if they ever get any of the wishes they make. And I don't know if there's enough magic in saying, "Rain, rain, go away; come again another day," so that the rain really *will* go away. But there certainly can be no harm in trying.

WINDS AND WEATHERS

When the wind is in the East,
'Tis neither good for man nor beast;
When the wind is in the North,
The skillful fisher goes not forth;
When the wind is in the South,
It blows the bait in the fishes' mouth;
When the wind is in the West,
Then 'tis at the very best.

The south wind brings wet weather;
The north wind wet and cold together;
The west wind always brings us rain;
The east wind blows it back again.

If the evening's red, and the morning gray,
It is the sign of a bonnie day;
If the evening's gray, and the morning red,
The lamb and the ewe will go wet to bed.

OLD COUNTRY RHYMES

THE WIND

Who has seen the wind?
   Neither I nor you;
But where the leaves hang trembling,
   The wind is passing through.

Who has seen the wind?
   Neither you nor I;
But when the trees bow down their heads,
   The wind is passing by.

CHRISTINA ROSSETTI

HAPPY WIND

Oh, happy wind, how sweet
   Thy life must be!
The great, proud fields of gold
   Run after thee!
And here are flowers, with heads
   To nod and shake;
And dreaming butterflies
   To tease and wake.
Oh, happy wind, I say,
To be alive this day.

W. H. DAVIES

WHENEVER THE WIND IS HIGH

WINDY NIGHTS

Whenever the moon and stars are set,
  Whenever the wind is high,
All night long in the dark and wet,
  A man goes riding by.
Late in the night when the fires are out,
Why does he gallop and gallop about?

Whenever the trees are crying aloud,
  And ships are tossed at sea,
By, on the highway, low and loud,
  By at the gallop goes he.
By at the gallop he goes, and then
By he comes back at the gallop again.

ROBERT LOUIS STEVENSON

TO THE THAWING WIND

Come with rain, O loud Southwester!
Bring the singer, bring the nester;
Give the buried flower a dream;
Make the settled snow-bank steam;
Find the brown beneath the white;
But whate'er you do tonight,
Bathe my window, make it flow,
Melt it as the ice will go;
Melt the glass and leave the sticks
Like a hermit's crucifix;

Burst into my narrow stall;
Swing the picture on the wall;
Run the rattling pages o'er;
Scatter poems on the floor;
Turn the poet out of door!

ROBERT FROST

THE CLOUD

I bring fresh showers for the thirsting flowers,
    From the seas and the streams;
I bear light shade for the leaves when laid
    In their noonday dreams.
From my wings are shaken the dews that waken
    The sweet buds every one,
When rocked to rest on their mother's breast,
    As she dances about the sun.
I wield the flail of the lashing hail,
    And whiten the green plains under,
And then again I dissolve it in rain,
    And laugh as I pass in thunder.

I sift the snow on the mountains below,
    And their great pines groan aghast;
And all the night 'tis my pillow white,
    While I sleep in the arms of the blast.
Sublime on the towers of my skiey bowers,
    Lightning my pilot sits;
In a cavern under is fettered the thunder,
    It struggles and howls at fits;
Over earth and ocean, with gentle motion,
    This pilot is guiding me,
Lured by the love of the genii that move
    In the depths of the purple sea;
Over the rills, and the crags, and the hills,

Over the lakes and the plains,
Wherever he dream, under mountain or stream,
The Spirit he loves remains;
And I all the while bask in Heaven's blue smile,
Whilst he is dissolving in rains.

PERCY BYSSHE SHELLEY

THE STORM

The other night before the storm
I sat and watched the rain-clouds swarm
Like great, black bees, so angry that
They buzzed with thunder. Well, I sat
And saw the wind come racing down,
Banging the shutters of the town;
Kicking the dust up in the road
And frightening every little toad.
He broke off branches for a toy,
Just like a large and wicked boy;
He threw the papers in the air,
And laughed as if he didn't care
What anyone might say or do.
He roared, and sang, and whistled, too.

Well, pretty soon things got so black
There was no sky except a crack,
One little streak of yellow light.
"See," father said, "just see how bright
The heavens shine behind it now;
And look, it seems to spread somehow."
But father didn't understand
That I had seen it—seen God's hand
When, in a flash, so sharp and sly,
He tore a hole in that black sky.

I guess God must have missed my face
Behind the clouds in that dark place,
And so He made a hole to see
Whatever had become of me.
Then, when the space grew red and wide
And full of gold, and father cried,
"Was ever such a brilliant hue,"
I only smiled because I knew
I had been looking in God's eye.
Yet I kept still, till by and by,
When father cried, "The lightning, see!"
I had to laugh out loud with glee,
For it was God that winked at me.

RICHARD AND LOUIS UNTERMEYER

THE STORM

We were waiting for the storm:
In the morning it was warm,

But the sky became so dark
That the tall trees in the park

Grew afraid, and started trembling.
Cloud on cloud began assembling.

In the middle of the day
Night came down and came to stay.

Thunder rumbled like a drum,
And we wondered what would come.

All at once, we don't know why,
Something happened in the sky.

Darkness fled, and it was light;
All the clouds blew out of sight,

And the sun was seen behind.
"God," said father, "changed His mind."

ROBIN CHRISTOPHER

SIGNS OF RAIN

The hollow winds begin to blow,
The clouds look black, the glass is low,
The soot falls down, the spaniels sleep,
The spiders from their cobwebs peep.
Last night the sun went pale to bed,
The moon in halos hid her head.
Hark how the chairs and tables crack!
Old Betty's joints are on the rack;
Loud quack the ducks, the peacocks cry;
The distant hills are seeming nigh.
How restless are the snorting swine;
The busy flies disturb the kine;
Low o'er the grass the swallow wings;
The cricket, too, how sharp he sings.
Puss on the hearth, with velvet paws,
Sits wiping o'er her whiskered jaws.
At dusk the squalid toad was seen,
Hopping and crawling o'er the green;
The whirling wind the dust obeys,
And in the rapid eddy plays.
The frog has changed his yellow vest,
And in a russet coat is dressed.
Though June, the air is cold and still,
The mellow blackbird's voice is shrill.
My dog, so altered in his taste,
Quits mutton-bones on grass to feast.
'Twill surely rain, I see with sorrow,
Our jaunt must be put off tomorrow.

E. JENNER

RAIN

Raining on earth
  Means weeping in heaven,
    My father once told me.

Maybe
  A baby-star
    Wandered too far . . .

Maybe the moon
  Stuck its head out too soon,
    And someone in space
      Scratched up its face.

Maybe the sun
  Was not feeling well.
    You never can tell.
      The sun is so old
        It may have caught cold.

Weeping in heaven
  Means raining on earth,
    My father once told me.

ROBIN CHRISTOPHER

THE RAIN

I hear leaves drinking rain;
  I hear rich leaves on top
Giving the poor beneath
  Drop after drop;
'Tis a sweet noise to hear
These green leaves drinking near.

And when the sun comes out,
  After this rain shall stop,
A wondrous light will fill
  Each dark, round drop;
I hope the sun shines bright;
'Twill be a lovely sight.

W. H. DAVIES

RAIN IN SUMMER

How beautiful is the rain!
After the dust and heat,
In the broad and fiery street,
In the narrow lane,
How beautiful is the rain!

How it clatters along the roofs,
Like the tramp of hoofs!
How it gushes and struggles out
From the throat of the overflowing spout!

Across the windowpane
It pours and pours;
And swift and wide,
With a muddy tide,
Like a river down the gutter roars
The rain, the welcome rain!

HENRY WADSWORTH LONGFELLOW

APRIL RAIN

It is not raining rain for me,
    It's raining daffodils;
In every dimpled drop I see
    Wild flowers on the hills.

The clouds of gray engulf the day
    And overwhelm the town;
It is not raining rain to me,
    It's raining roses down.

A health unto the happy,
    A fig for him who frets!
It is not raining rain to me,
    It's raining violets.

ROBERT LOVEMAN

WRITTEN IN MARCH

The cock is crowing,
The stream is flowing,
The small birds twitter,
The lake doth glitter,
The green field sleeps in the sun;
    The oldest and youngest
    Are at work with the strongest;

171

The cattle are grazing,
Their heads never raising;
There are forty feeding like one!

Like an army defeated
The snow hath retreated,
And now doth fare ill
On the top of the bare hill;
The plowboy is whooping—anon—anon:
There's joy in the mountains;
There's life in the fountains;
Small clouds are sailing,
Blue sky prevailing;
The rain is over and gone!

WILLIAM WORDSWORTH

MAY DAY

Good morning, lords and ladies, it is the first of May;
We hope you'll view our garland, it is so sweet and gay.

The cuckoo sings in April, the cuckoo sings in May,
The cuckoo sings in June, in July she flies away.

The cuckoo drinks cold water to make her sing so clear.
And then she sings "Cuckoo! Cuckoo!" for three months in the year.

I love my little brother and sister every day,
But I seem to love them better in the merry month of May.

OLD SONG

SPRING

Now that the winter's gone, the earth hath lost
Her snow-white robes; and now no more the frost
Candies the grass or casts an icy cream
Upon the silver lake or crystal stream;
But the warm sun thaws the benumbèd earth,
And makes it tender; gives a sacred birth
To the dead swallow; wakes in hollow tree
The drowsy cuckoo and the bumble-bee.
Now do a choir of chirping minstrels bring
In triumph to the world the youthful spring!
The valleys, hills, and woods, in rich array,
Welcome the coming of the longed-for May.

THOMAS CAREW

SPRING

Spring, the sweet Spring, is the year's pleasant king;
Then blooms each thing, then maids dance in a ring,
Cold doth not sting, the pretty birds do sing,
    Cuckoo, jug-jug, pu-we, to-witta-woo!

The palm and may make country houses gay,
Lambs frisk and play, the shepherds pipe all day,
And we hear aye birds tune this merry lay,
    Cuckoo, jug-jug, pu-we, to-witta-woo!

Rainbow in the Sky

The fields breathe sweet, the daisies kiss our feet,
Young lovers meet, old wives a-sunning sit,
In every street these tunes our ears do greet,
Cuckoo, jug-jug, pu-we, to-witta-woo!

THOMAS NASHE

SPRING

Sound the Flute!
Now it's mute.
Birds delight
Day and Night;
Nightingale
In the dale,
Lark in Sky,
Merrily,
Merrily, Merrily, to welcome in the Year.

Little Boy
Full of joy,
Little Girl
Sweet and small,
Cock does crow,
So do you;
Merry voice,
Infant noise,
Merrily, Merrily, to welcome in the Year.

Little Lamb
Here I am,
Come and lick
My white neck,
Let me pull
Your soft Wool,
Let me kiss
Your soft face;
Merrily, Merrily, we welcome in the Year.

WILLIAM BLAKE

SPRING

I wander far and unrestrained,
Myself set free, my fields regained,
    When in the Spring,
    The South winds sing,
And I by birds am entertained.

JOHN ALDEN CARPENTER

BED IN SUMMER

In winter I get up at night
And dress by yellow candle-light.
In summer, quite the other way,
I have to go to bed by day.

I have to go to bed and see
The birds still hopping on the tree,
Or hear the grown-up people's feet
Still going past me in the street.

175

And does it not seem hard to you,
When all the sky is clear and blue,
And I should like so much to play,
To have to go to bed by day?

ROBERT LOUIS STEVENSON

SUMMER

The cock's on the housetop blowing his horn;
The bull's in the barn, a-threshing of corn;
The maid's in the meadow, a-making of hay;
The ducks in the river are swimming away.

OLD RHYME

SNOW

White bird, featherless,
Flew from Paradise,
Perched on the castle wall.
Poor Lord Landless
Came in a fine dress,
And went away without a dress at all.

OLD RHYME

OCTOBER'S PARTY

October gave a party;
The leaves by hundreds came—
The Chestnuts, Oaks, and Maples,
And leaves of every name.
The Sunshine spread a carpet,
And everything was grand,
Miss Weather led the dancing,
Professor Wind the band.

The Chestnuts came in yellow,
　　The Oaks in crimson dressed;
The lovely Misses Maple
　　In scarlet looked their best;
All balanced to their partners,
　　And gayly fluttered by;
The sight was like a rainbow
　　New fallen from the sky.

Then, in the rustic hollow,
　　At hide-and-seek they played,
The party closed at sundown,
　　And everybody stayed.
Professor Wind played louder;
　　They flew along the ground;
And then the party ended
　　In jolly "Hands Around."

GEORGE COOPER

NOVEMBER

No sun—no moon—
No morn—no noon—
No dawn—no dusk—no proper time of day—
No sky—no earthly view—
No distance looking blue—
No road—no street—no "t'other side the way"—
No end to any row—
No indications where the crescents go—
No top to any steeple—
No recognitions of familiar people—
No courtesies for showing 'em—
No knowing 'em!

177

No traveling at all—no locomotion—
No inkling of the way—no notion—
"No go"—by land or ocean—
No mail—no post—
No news from any foreign coast—
No park—no ring—no afternoon gentility—
No company—no nobility—
No warmth, no cheerfulness, no healthful ease,
No comfortable feel in any member—
No shade, no shine, no butterflies, no bees—
November!

THOMAS HOOD

THE FROST

The Frost looked forth, one still, clear night,
And he said, "Now I shall be out of sight;
So through the valley and over the height
   In silence I'll take my way.
I will not go like that blustering train,
The wind and the snow, the hail and the rain,
Who make so much bustle and noise in vain,
   But I'll be as busy as they!"

Then he went to the mountain and powdered its crest,
He climbed up the trees and their boughs he dressed
With diamonds and pearls, and over the breast
   Of the quivering lake he spread
A coat of mail, that it need not fear
The downward point of many a spear
That he hung on its margin, far and near,
   Where a rock could rear its head.

He went to the windows of those who slept,
And over each pane like a fairy crept;

Wherever he breathed, wherever he stepped,
  By the light of the moon were seen
Most beautiful things. There were flowers and trees,
There were bevies of birds and swarms of bees,
There were cities, thrones, temples, and towers, and these
  All pictured in silver sheen!

But he did one thing that was hardly fair,—
He peeped in the cupboard and finding there
That all had forgotten for him to prepare,—
  Now, just to set them a-thinking,
"I'll bite this basket of fruit," said he;
"This costly pitcher I'll burst in three,
And the glass of water they've left for me
  Shall *tchick!* to tell them I'm drinking."

HANNAH FLAGG GOULD

THE MONTHS

January brings the snow,
Makes our feet and fingers glow.

February brings the rain,
Thaws the frozen lake again.

March brings breezes loud and shrill,
Stirs the dancing daffodil.

April brings the primrose sweet,
Scatters daisies at our feet.

May brings flocks of pretty lambs,
Skipping by their fleecy dams.

June brings tulips, lilies, roses,
Fills the children's hands with posies.

Hot July brings cooling showers,
Apricots and gillyflowers.

August brings the sheaves of corn,
Then the harvest home is borne.

Warm September brings the fruit,
Sportsmen then begin to shoot.

Fresh October brings the pheasant,
Then to gather nuts is pleasant.

Dull November brings the blast,
Then the leaves are whirling fast.

Chill December brings the sleet,
Blazing fire and Christmas treat.

SARA COLERIDGE

THE MONTHS

January cold desolate;
February dripping wet;
March wind ranges;
April changes;
Birds sing in tune
To flowers of May,
And sunny June
Brings longest day;
In scorched July
The storm-clouds fly,
Lightning-torn;
August bears corn,
September fruit;
In rough October
Earth must disrobe her;
Stars fall and shoot
In keen November;
And night is long
And cold is strong
In bleak December.

CHRISTINA ROSSETTI

SIGNS AND SEASONS

Rain before seven,
Clear before eleven.

March winds and April showers
Bring forth May flowers.

Rainbow at night
Is the sailor's delight.
Rainbow at morning,
Sailors take warning!

A swarm of bees in May
Is worth a load of hay;
A swarm of bees in June
Is worth a silver spoon.
A swarm of bees in July
Is not worth a fly.

A sunshiny shower
Won't last an hour.

St. Swithin's Day, if thou dost rain,
    For forty days it will remain;
St. Swithin's Day, if thou be fair,
    For forty days 'twill rain na mair.

When the days begin to lengthen,
Then the cold begins to strengthen.

March brings the lamb,
   And buds the thorn,
But blows through the flint
   Of an ox's horn.

Under the heather
   Is hunger and cold;
Under the broom
   Is silver and gold.

In the month of April,
   When green leaves begin to spring,
Little lambs do skip like fairies,
   Birds do couple, build, and sing.

Winter's thunder
Is the world's wonder.

If bees stay at home,
Rain will soon come.

If they fly away
Fine will be the day.

OLD WIVES' SAYINGS

If you sneeze on Monday, you sneeze for danger;
Sneeze on a Tuesday, kiss a stranger;
Sneeze on Wednesday, sneeze for a letter;
Sneeze on a Thursday, something better;
Sneeze on a Friday, sneeze for sorrow;
Sneeze on a Saturday, see your sweetheart tomorrow.

Go to bed first,
A golden purse;
Go to bed second,
A golden pheasant;
Go to bed third,
A golden bird.

See a pin and pick it up,
All the day you'll have good luck.
See a pin and let it lay,
You'll have bad luck all the day.

CHARMS

Load of hay!
Load of hay!
Make a wish
And turn away!

Star-light, star-bright,
First star I see tonight;
I wish I may, I wish I might,
Get the wish I wish tonight.

Rain, rain, go away;
Come again another day.
Little Mary wants to play.

Hiccup, sniccup,
Rise up, right up;
Three drops from the wine-cup
Are sure to stop the hiccup.

Peter Piper picked a peck of pickled peppers;
A peck of pickled peppers Peter Piper picked;
If Peter Piper picked a peck of pickled peppers,
Where's the peck of pickled peppers Peter Piper picked?

STAR-LIGHT, STAR-BRIGHT

IN HEAVEN AND EARTH

IN HEAVEN AND EARTH

"Heaven," says the poet, "lies about us in our infancy," and poetry lies about us at all times, in the depths of the sea, on the peaks of the hills, in heaven and earth, everywhere. Under your feet the buttercups and daisies, over your head the moon and stars make poems for your pleasure.

Flowers have always had a language of their own and poets have always tried to translate it. Hundreds of years ago some unknown poet saw the spring daffodil as a lady coming up to town "in yellow petticoat and a green gown," and a living poet sees the dandelions as half-lions, half-daisies, "with yellow manes."

So with everything in nature. Some may see a running brook as nothing more than a waste of water; but Tennyson sees it skipping and sliding, bubbling and babbling, eternal as the earth from which it flows—"for men may come and men may go, but I go on forever." Longfellow discovers the depths in a far greater expanse of water, and discloses the secret of the sea.

The simplest things take on a glory—the "glory of the commonplace"—when seen with the poetic eye. In "A Wish" Samuel Rogers pictures an ordinary cottage with its ivy-covered porch, and all the details—from the swallow's nest beneath the roof to the old spinning wheel—stand out with beauty and dignity. Even the milkmen, in Robin Christopher's "One, Two, Three," have an air of magic as they come out of the dawn with daybreak and the birds.

Night, the slow coming-on of the dark, the gradual appearance of the stars, the rising of the harvest moon, and the flooding of full moonlight have always made men look at the heavens with wonder. This section contains a few poems that show how these wonders have affected different poets.

CONTEMPLATION

For days and days I've climbed a tree,
    A dappled yellow tree,
And gazed abroad at many things
    I've always wished to see.

I see the green and gentle fields
    All bounded in with hedge,
And shining river swimming through
    The rushes on his edge.

And little sheep who play all day,
    I watch them as they run,
While far away the roofs of town
    Are shining in the sun.

I think it's very nice to sit
    So high and look so far . . .
How very large the world can be!
    How many things there are!

JOHN ALDEN CARPENTER

ONE, TWO, THREE

Out of the earth come good things,
  And out of the sky, the sun;
And out of the clock the minutes
  Come one,
  By one,
  By one.

Out of the day the night comes,
  And out of the darkening blue
The twink-a-ling red and gold stars
  Come two,
  By two,
  By two.

Out of the east the dawn comes,
  And birds come out of the tree;
And out of the distance, milkmen
  Come three,
  By three,
  By three.

ROBIN CHRISTOPHER

A WISH

Mine be a cot beside the hill;
A beehive's hum shall soothe my ear;
A willowy brook that turns a mill,
With many a fall shall linger near.

The swallow oft, beneath my thatch,
Shall twitter from her clay-built nest;
Oft shall the pilgrim lift the latch,
And share my meal, a welcome guest.

Around my ivied porch shall spring
Each fragrant flower that drinks the dew;
And Lucy, at her wheel, shall sing
In russet gown and apron blue.

The village church, among the trees,
Where first our marriage-vows were given,
With merry peals shall swell the breeze,
And point with taper spire to heaven.

SAMUEL ROGERS

OLD GARDEN RHYMES

A Tree

In Spring I look gay,
Decked in comely array,
In summer more clothing I wear;
When colder it grows
I fling off my clothes,
And in winter quite naked appear.

Spring Flower

Daffy-down-dilly has come up to town
In yellow petticoat and a green gown.

Flower Tokens

Lilies are white,
Rosemary's green;
When you are king,
I shall be queen.

Roses are red,
Lavender's blue;
If you will have me,
I will have you.

ROSES ARE RED

Roses are red,
Violets blue;
Pinks are sweet—
And so are you!

BUTTERCUPS

Buttercups, buttercups
  Stretching for miles
Through the green meadow-land,
  Over the stiles.

Buttercups, buttercups,
  Standing so high
In all the summer grass,
  Under the sky.

DOLLY RADFORD

DAISIES

Where innocent bright-eyed daisies are,
  With blades of grass between,
Each daisy stands up like a star,
  Out of a sky of green.

CHRISTINA ROSSETTI

DANDELIONS

These lions, each by a daisy queen,
With yellow manes, and golden mien,
Keep so still for wind to start
They stare, like eyes that have no smart.
But, once they hear that shepherd pipe,
Down meadows and through orchards ripe,
They dance together, lion and daisy,
Through long midday, slow and lazy.
Now by night winds roughly kissed
His mane becomes a clock of mist,
Which mortal breath next morn will blow,
While his white virgins bloom below.

SACHEVERELL SITWELL

COME, LITTLE LEAVES

"Come, little leaves," said the wind one day,
"Come o'er the meadows with me and play;
Put on your dresses of red and gold,
For summer is gone and the days grow cold."

Soon as the leaves heard the wind's loud call,
Down they came fluttering, one and all;
Over the brown fields they danced and flew,
Singing the glad little songs they knew.

"Cricket, good-by, we've been friends so long,
Little brook, sing us your farewell song;
Say you are sorry to see us go;
Ah, you will miss us, right well we know.

"Dear little lambs in your fleecy fold,
Mother will keep you from harm and cold;
Fondly we watched you in vale and glade,
Say, will you dream of our loving shade?"

Dancing and whirling, the little leaves went,
Winter had called them, and they were content;
Soon, fast asleep in their earthy beds,
The snow laid a coverlid over their heads.

GEORGE COOPER

THE IVY GREEN

Oh, a dainty plant is the Ivy green,
That creepeth o'er ruins old!
Of right choice food are his meals, I ween,
In his cell so lone and cold.
The wall must be crumbled, the stone decayed,
To pleasure his dainty whim:
And the moldering dust that years have made
Is a merry meal for him.
   Creeping where no life is seen,
   A rare old plant is the Ivy green.

Fast he stealeth on, though he wears no wings,
And a staunch old heart has he.
How closely he twineth, how tight he clings
To his friend the huge Oak Tree!

197

And slyly he traileth along the ground,
And his leaves he gently waves,
As he joyously hugs and crawleth round
The rich mold of dead men's graves.
    Creeping where grim death has been,
    A rare old plant is the Ivy green.

Whole ages have fled and their works decayed,
And nations have scattered been;
But the stout old Ivy shall never fade
From its hale and hearty green.
The brave old plant in its lonely days,
Shall fatten upon the past:
For the stateliest building man can raise,
Is the Ivy's food at last.
    Creeping on where time has been,
    A rare old plant is the Ivy green.

                              CHARLES DICKENS

THE GREENWOOD TREE

Under the greenwood tree
Who loves to lie with me,
And tune his merry note
Unto the sweet bird's throat—
Come hither, come hither, come hither!
    Here shall he see
    No enemy
But winter and rough weather.

                              WILLIAM SHAKESPEARE

THE PEPPER TREE

On a night the sun and the earth and the weather
And their brother, the wind, all slept together.

And it happened while they were slumbering
That each one dreamed of a different thing,

And then awoke.
The wind first spoke.

"I dreamed," said he,
"Of a fairy tree."

"And I," said the weather,
"Of a fairy's feather."

Spoke the earth, "My dream
Was all agleam

"With rubies red
Of fairies." Said

The sun, "Mine made
A fairy glade
Of delicately woven shade."

Then they laughed, did the sun and the earth and the weather
And the wind, as they put their dreams together.

But I wonder if ever these gay lads knew
That the pepper tree on that same night grew.

SISTER M. MADELEVA

THE BROOK

I come from haunts of coot and hern,[1]
    I make a sudden sally
And sparkle out among the fern,
    To bicker down a valley.

By thirty hills I hurry down,
    Or slip between the ridges,
By twenty thorps,[2] a little town,
    And half a hundred bridges.

Till last by Philip's farm I flow
    To join the brimming river,
For men may come and men may go,
    But I go on for ever.

I chatter over stony ways,
    In little sharps and trebles,
I bubble into eddying bays,
    I babble on the pebbles.

With many a curve my banks I fret
    By many a field and fallow,
And many a fairy foreland set
    With willow-weed and mallow.

I chatter, chatter, as I flow
    To join the brimming river,
For men may come and men may go,
    But I go on for ever.

[1] Coot and hern: water-birds.   [2] Thorps: small villages.

I wind about, and in and out,
   With here a blossom sailing,
And here and there a lusty trout,
   And here and there a grayling,

And here and there a foamy flake
   Upon me, as I travel
With many a silvery waterbreak
   Above the golden gravel.

I steal by lawns and grassy plots,
   I slide by hazel covers;
I move the sweet forget-me-nots
   That grow for happy lovers.

I slip, I slide, I gloom, I glance,
   Among my skimming swallows;
I make the netted sunbeam dance
   Against my sandy shallows.

I murmur under moon and stars
   In brambly wildernesses;
I linger by my shingly bars;
   I loiter round my cresses;

And out again I curve and flow
   To join the brimming river,
For men may come and men may go,
   But I go on for ever.

         ALFRED, LORD TENNYSON

THE SECRET OF THE SEA

Ah! what pleasant visions haunt me
   As I gaze upon the sea!
All the old romantic legends,
   All my dreams, come back to me.

Rainbow in the Sky

Sails of silk and ropes of sendal,[1]
   Such as gleam in ancient lore;
And the singing of the sailors,
   And the answer from the shore!

Most of all, the Spanish ballad
   Haunts me oft, and tarries long,
Of the noble Count Arnaldos
   And the sailor's mystic song.

Like the long waves on a sea-beach,
   Where the sand as silver shines,
With a soft, monotonous cadence,
   Flow its unrhymed lyric lines;—

Telling how the Count Arnaldos,
   With his hawk upon his hand,
Saw a fair and stately galley,
   Steering onward to the land;—

How he heard the ancient helmsman
   Chant a song so wild and clear,
That the sailing sea-bird slowly
   Poised upon the mast to hear,

Till his soul was full of longing,
   And he cried, with impulse strong,—
"Helmsman! for the love of heaven,
   Teach me, too, that wondrous song!"

"Wouldst thou,"—so the helmsman answered,
   "Learn the secret of the sea?
Only those who brave its dangers
   Comprehend its mystery!"

In each sail that skims the horizon,
   In each landward-blowing breeze,

[1] Sendal: thin silky material.

I behold that stately galley,
    Hear those mournful melodies;

Till my soul is full of longing
    For the secret of the sea,
And the heart of the great ocean
    Sends a thrilling pulse through me.

HENRY WADSWORTH LONGFELLOW

UPON A HILL

I stood tiptoe upon a little hill;
The air was cooling, and so very still
That the sweet buds which with a modest pride
Pull droopingly, in slanting curve aside,
Their scanty-leaved and finely-tapering stems,
Had not yet lost their starry diadems
Caught from the early sobbing of the morn.
The clouds were pure and white as flocks new-shorn,
And fresh from the clear brook; sweetly they slept
On the blue fields of heaven, and then there crept
A little noiseless noise among the leaves,
Born of the very sigh that silence heaves;
For not the faintest motion could be seen
Of all the shades that slanted o'er the green.
There was wide wand'ring for the greediest eye
To peer about upon variety;
Far round the horizon's crystal air to skim,
And trace the dwindled edgings of its brim;
To picture out the quaint and curious bending
Of the fresh woodland alley never-ending;
Or by the bowery clefts and leafy shelves,
Guess where the jaunty streams refresh themselves.

JOHN KEATS

LIGHT THE LAMPS UP, LAMPLIGHTER

LIGHT THE LAMPS UP, LAMPLIGHTER

Light the lamps up, Lamplighter,
The people are in the street—
   Without a light
   They have no sight,
And where will they plant their feet?
Some will tread in the gutter,
And some in the mud—oh dear!
Light the lamps up, Lamplighter,
Because the night is here.

Light the candles, Grandmother,
The children are going to bed—
   Without a wick
   They'll stumble and stick,
And where will they lay their head?

Some will lie on the staircase,
And some in the hearth—oh dear!
Light the candles, Grandmother,
Because the night is here.

Light the stars up, Gabriel,
The cherubs are out to fly—
   If heaven is blind
   How will they find
Their way across the sky?
Some will splash in the Milky Way,
Or bump on the moon—oh dear!
Light the stars up, Gabriel,
Because the night is here.

ELEANOR FARJEON

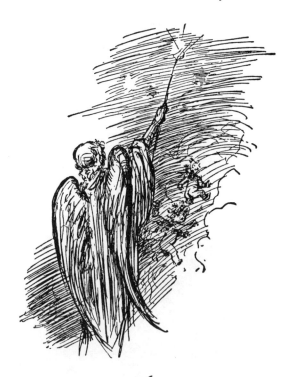

QUESTIONS AT NIGHT

Why
Is the sky?

What starts the thunder overhead?
Who makes the crashing noise?
Are the angels falling out of bed?
Are they breaking all their toys?

Why does the sun go down so soon?
Why do the night-clouds crawl
Hungrily up to the new-laid moon
And swallow it, shell and all?

If there's a Bear among the stars,
As all the people say,
Won't he jump over those Pasture-bars
And drink up the Milky Way?

Does every star that happens to fall
Turn into a fire-fly?
Can't it ever get back to Heaven at all?

And why
Is the sky?

LOUIS UNTERMEYER

THE STAR

Twinkle, twinkle, little star,
How I wonder what you are!
Up above the world so high,
Like a diamond in the sky.

When the blazing sun is gone,
When he nothing shines upon,
Then you show your little light,
Twinkle, twinkle, all the night.

Then the traveler in the dark
Thanks you for your tiny spark;
He could not see which way to go,
If you did not twinkle so.

In the dark blue sky you keep,
And often through my curtains peep,
For you never shut your eye
Till the sun is in the sky.

As your bright and tiny spark
Lights the traveler in the dark,
Though I know not what you are,
Twinkle, twinkle, little star.

ANN and JANE TAYLOR

THE MOON

O, look at the moon!
  She is shining up there;
O mother, she looks
  Like a lamp in the air.

Last week she was smaller,
  And shaped like a bow;
But now she's grown bigger,
  And round as an O.

Pretty moon, pretty moon,
  How you shine on the door,
And make it all bright
  On my nursery floor!

You shine on my playthings,
  And show me their place,
And I love to look up
  At your pretty face.

And there is a star
  Close by you, and maybe
That small twinkling star
  Is *your* little baby.

ELIZA LEE FOLLEN

YOUNG NIGHT-THOUGHT

All night long and every night
When my mamma puts out the light,
I see the people marching by,
As plain as day, before my eye.

Armies and emperors and kings,
All carrying different kinds of things,
And marching in so grand a way,
You never saw the like by day.

So fine a show was never seen
At the great circus on the green;
For every kind of beast and man
Is marching in that caravan.

At first they move a little slow,
But soon the faster on they go,
And still beside them close I keep
Until we reach the town of Sleep.

ROBERT LOUIS STEVENSON

NIGHT

The sun descending in the west,
   The evening star does shine;
The birds are silent in their nest,
   And I must seek for mine.
The moon, like a flower,
In heaven's high bower,
With silent delight
Sits and smiles on the night.

Farewell, green fields and happy groves,
   Where flocks have took delight.
Where lambs have nibbled, silent moves
   The feet of angels bright;
Unseen they pour blessing,
And joy without ceasing,
On each bud and blossom,
And each sleeping bosom.

              WILLIAM BLAKE

EARLY MORNING

The moon on the one hand, the dawn on the other:
The moon is my sister, the dawn is my brother.
The moon on my left hand the dawn on my right:
My brother, good morning: my sister, good night.

              HILAIRE BELLOC

FIN, FUR, AND FEATHER

FIN, FUR, AND FEATHER

Here, as you probably have guessed, are poems about things that swim, fly, leap, walk, creep and crawl. Here you will find creatures of the thick woods and the open fields, of the mountaintop and the sea, creatures as wild as the eagle and as tame as the house-cat—even the quiet oyster is here.

The section begins with several poems about the robin, that cheerful bird who is as much at home on our lawns as he is in the forest. Very likely you know some of these verses, for they are quite old, older than Mother Goose herself, so old that no one knows who wrote them. Then come more bird-poems—poems about the wren, and the dove, and the cuckoo, and the cock, and the crow, and the wagtail (that brisk little bird with a long tail which he is always wagging), and the nightingale, and the lark (the poet's own bird), the barn-swallow, the blackbird, the owl, the eagle, and that horrid bird of prey (only here he is rather humorous) the vulture. Many of the poems about these birds will, I think, be new to you, and many have been written by such great poets as Shakespeare and Christina Rossetti and Tennyson.

But, though the poets seem to admire birds more than any other of God's creatures, there are plenty of poems about other animals as well. Dorothy Aldis writes charmingly about the farm animals who grow heavier coats as cold weather comes on. William Blake's "The Lamb" is one of the tenderest poems ever written, and Mrs. Hale's "Mary's Lamb" is even more famous. You will find the dog here, described by two Olivers—Oliver Herford and Oliver Gold-smith—and both descriptions are comic. As for cats—! Oliver Herford has written a whole book about them in imitation of Robert Louis Stevenson's, and he calls it "A Kitten's Garden of Verses." Here you will find poems about the fireside pet—someone has called it "The Tiger in the House"—as modern as Emma Rounds' burlesque of the old nursery rhyme on page 232, and a poem about an Irish student and his cat which is over a thousand years old—I mean the poem is over a thousand years old, not the cat. Margaret Widdemer's "The

215

Willow Cats" is about another kind of kitten; it's about a kitten with a bark; not, strictly speaking, a kitten at all. And, as near the cat-poem as may be safe, is Elizabeth Coatsworth's "The Mouse," a poem that makes us far more sympathetic to mice than we usually are.

Greater animals are here, too! Hilaire Belloc's "The Baboon" and "The Rhinoceros," both of them large and laughable. And, toward the end of the group, are poems about quite different classes of living things—insects, and frogs, and butterflies, and turtles and dolphins, and various fishes, and dancing lobsters, and barnacles that build themselves houses on the bottoms of boats. And, to end with, there are beasts so queerly mixed that they never lived except in a poet's mind. And a very good thing that is!

THE ROBIN

Little Robin Redbreast
Sat upon a tree,
He sang merrily,
As merrily as could be.

He nodded with his head,
And his tail waggled he,
As little Robin Redbreast
Sat upon a tree.

The North Wind doth blow,
And we shall have snow
And what will poor Robin do then, poor thing?

He'll sit in the barn,
And keep himself warm,
And hide his head under his wing, poor thing.

Cock Robin got up early
At the break of day,
And went to Jenny's window
To sing a roundelay.

He sang Cock Robin's love
To little Jenny Wren,
And when he got unto the end,
Then he began again.

Little Robin-Redbreast sat upon a tree;
Up went Pussy cat, and down went he;
Down came Pussy cat, and away Robin ran:
Says little Robin-Redbreast, "Catch me if you can."
Little Robin-Redbreast jumped upon a wall;
Pussy cat jumped after him and almost got a fall;
Little Robin chirped and sang, and what did Pussy say?
Pussy cat said "Mew," and Robin jumped away.

DEATH AND BURIAL OF COCK ROBIN

Who killed Cock Robin?
    "I," said the Sparrow,
    "With my bow and arrow,
I killed Cock Robin."

Who saw him die?
    "I," said the Fly,
    "With my little eye,
I saw him die."

Who caught his blood?
    "I," said the Fish,
    "With my little dish,
I caught his blood."

Who'll make his shroud?
    "I," said the Beetle,
    "With my thread and needle,
I'll make his shroud."

Who'll dig his grave?
    "I," said the Owl,
    "With my spade and trowel,
I'll dig his grave."

Who'll be the parson?
  "I," said the Rook,
  "With my little book.
I'll be the parson."

Who'll be the clerk?
  "I," said the Lark,
  "I'll say Amen in the dark;
I'll be the clerk."

Who'll be chief mourner?
  "I," said the Dove,
  "I mourn for my love;
I'll be chief mourner."

Who'll bear the torch?
  "I," said the Linnet,
  "I'll come in a minute,
I'll bear the torch."

Who'll sing his dirge?
  "I," said the thrush,
  "As I sing in the bush
I'll sing his dirge."

Who'll bear the pall?
  "We," said the Wren,
  Both the cock and the hen;
"We'll bear the pall."

Who'll carry his coffin?
  "I," said the Kite
  "If it be in the night,
I'll carry his coffin."

Who'll toll the bell?
"I," said the Bull,
"Because I can pull,
I'll toll the bell."

All the birds of the air
Fell to sighing and sobbing
When they heard the bell toll
For poor Cock Robin.

P. S.

To all it concerns,
This notice apprises,
The Sparrow's for trial,
At next bird assizes.

THE DOVE AND THE WREN

The Dove
"Coo, coo, coo,
Me and my poor two;
Two sticks across,
And a bit of moss,
And it must do, do, do."

The Wren
"Pooh, pooh, pooh,
That will never do!
Look," says the wren,
"I've got ten,
And keep them all like gentlemen."

THE CUCKOO

The cuckoo's a fine bird
  He sings as he flies;
He brings us good tidings,
  He tells us no lies.

He sucks little birds' eggs
  To make his voice clear;
And when he sings "Cuckoo!"
  The summer is near.

Cuckoo, Cuckoo,
What do you do?

In April
I open my bill.

In May
I sing all day.

In June
I change my tune.

In July
Away I fly

In August
Away I must!

CRUEL JENNY WREN

Jenny Wren fell sick,
   Upon a merry time.
In came Robin-Redbreast
   And brought her sops and wine.

"Eat well of the sops, Jenny,
   Drink well of the wine."
"Thank you, Robin, kindly,
   You shall be mine."

Jenny she got well,
   And stood upon her feet,
And told Robin plainly,
   She loved him not a bit.

Robin, being angry,
   Hopped upon a twig,
Saying, "Out upon you! Fie upon you!
   Bold-faced jig!"

ANY BIRD

I haven't a palace,
I haven't a throne,
There isn't a thing
In the world I own.

I bathe in the bird-bath,
I perch on the trees;
I come and I go
Whenever I please.

But everyone's garden
Is open and free,
There's always a crumb
Or a worm there for me.

I fly where I will,
By woodland or sea;
The whole world is mine;
I'm rich as can be!

ILO ORLEANS

THE BROWN THRUSH

There's a merry brown thrush sitting up in the tree.
"He's singing to me! He's singing to me!"
And what does he say, little girl, little boy?
"Oh, the world's running over with joy!
　　Don't you hear? Don't you see?
　　Hush! Look! In my tree,
　　I'm as happy as happy can be!"

And the brown thrush keeps singing, "A nest do you see,
And five eggs, hid by me in the juniper-tree?
Don't meddle. Don't touch, little girl, little boy,
Or the world will lose some of its joy.
　　Now I'm glad! Now I'm free!
　　And I always shall be,
　　If you never bring sorrow to me."

So the merry brown thrush sings away in the tree,
To you and to me, to you and to me;
And he sings all the day, little girl, little boy,
"Oh, the world's running over with joy!
　　But long it won't be,
　　(Don't you know? Don't you see?)
　　Unless we're as good as can be."

LUCY LARCOM

THE COCK

Strutting cock with swelling chest,
   Stepping on your scaly legs,
Past the warm and busy nest
   Where the worried hens lay eggs,
Why do *you*, I'd like to know,
Strut and crow and swagger so.

Do you really think, I beg,
   When the sun swims into view,
That it is a yellow egg
   Which has just been laid by you?
While your poor wives cackle tunes,
Only laying little moons.

ELEANOR FARJEON

THE COCKS

Cocks crow in the morn
To tell us to rise,
And he who lies late
Will never be wise.

For early to bed
And early to rise
Is the way to be healthy,
And wealthy, and wise.

THE CROWS

On the first of March
The crows begin to search;
By the first of April
They are sitting still;
By the first of May
They've all flown away;
Coming greedy back again
With October's wind and rain.

LITTLE TROTTY WAGTAIL

Little trotty wagtail, he went in the rain,
And twittering, tottering sideways he ne'er got straight again.
He stooped to get a worm, and looked up to get a fly,
And then he flew away ere his feathers they were dry.

Little trotty wagtail, he waddled in the mud,
And left his little footmarks, trample where he would.
He waddled in the water-pudge, and waggle went his tail,
And chirrupt up his wings to dry upon the garden rail

Little trotty wagtail, you nimble all about,
And in the dimpling water-pudge you waddle in and out;
Your home is nigh at hand, and in the warm pig-stye,
So, little Master Wagtail, I'll bid you a good-by.

JOHN CLARE

SKYLARK AND NIGHTINGALE

When a mounting skylark sings
    In the sunlit summer morn,
I know that heaven is up on high,
    And on earth are fields of corn.

But when a nightingale sings
    In the moonlit summer even,
I know not if earth is merely earth,
    Only that heaven is heaven.
                  CHRISTINA ROSSETTI

THE LARK

Hark! hark! the lark at heaven's gate sings,
    And Phoebus[1] 'gins arise,
His steeds to water at those springs
    On chaliced flowers that lies;
And winking Mary-buds begin
    To ope their golden eyes;
With every thing that pretty is,
    My lady sweet, arise;
        Arise, arise!
                  WILLIAM SHAKESPEARE

[1] Phoebus: the sun.

THE BARN-SWALLOW

In the Allegheny Mountains
   When the apple orchards bloom
I know of eaves in a big red barn
   Where I'll find nesting room.

I'm coming back! I'm coming back!
   My wings are on the wind;
I'm coming back with the spring-time
   To the hills I've left behind.

I'm coming back! I'm coming back!
   To the hills that I know best,
Where the mountains sleep, and the winds walk,
   And where my wings can rest.

WILLIAM SARGENT

ONE BLACKBIRD

The stars must make an awful noise
In whirling round the sky;
Yet somehow I can't even hear
Their loudest song or sigh.

So it is wonderful to think
One blackbird can outsing
The voice of all the swarming stars
On any day in Spring.

HAROLD MONRO

227

THE OWL

When cats run home and light is come,
  And dew is cold upon the ground,
And the far-off stream is dumb,
  And the whirring sail goes round,
  And the whirring sail goes round:
    Alone and warming his five wits,
    The white owl in the belfry sits.

When merry milkmaids click the latch,
  And rarely smells the new-mown hay,
And the cock hath sung beneath the thatch
  Twice or thrice his roundelay,
  Twice or thrice his roundelay:
    Alone and warming his five wits,
    The white owl in the belfry sits.

ALFRED, LORD TENNYSON

THE EAGLE

He clasps the crag with crooked hands;
Close to the sun in lonely lands,
Ringed with the azure world, he stands.

The wrinkled sea beneath him crawls;
He watches from his mountain walls,
And like a thunderbolt he falls.

ALFRED, LORD TENNYSON

THE VULTURE

The Vulture eats between his meals,
   And that's the reason why
He very, very rarely feels
   As well as you and I.

His eye is dull, his head is bald,
   His neck is growing thinner.
Oh! What a lesson for us all
   To only eat at dinner!

HILAIRE BELLOC

THE BIG BABOON

The Big Baboon is found upon
   The plains of Cariboo;
He goes about with nothing on
   (A shocking thing to do).

But if he dressed respectably
   And let his whiskers grow,
How like this Big Baboon would be
   To Mister So-and-so!

HILAIRE BELLOC

THE VIPER

Yet another great truth I record in my verse,
That some vipers are venomous, some the reverse;
   As fact you may prove if you try,
By procuring two vipers and letting them bite:
With the *first* you are only the worse for a fright,
   But after the *second* you die.

HILAIRE BELLOC

WINTER COATS

In October, when they know
That very soon there will be snow,

Cows and horses, sheep and goats
Start to grow their winter coats.

Each year they grow them, fine and new,
(And fitting very nicely too),
But with no buttons to undo,

Nor pockets for a handkerchief.
And so they have to snort and sniff.

DOROTHY ALDIS

THE PONY

I had a little pony,
His name was Dapple-gray;
I lent him to a lady
To ride a mile away.

She whipped him, she slashed him,
She rode him through the mire.
I would not lend my pony now
For all the lady's hire.

NURSERY RHYME

THE RHINOCEROS

Rhinoceros, your hide looks all undone,
You do not take my fancy in the least;
You have a horn where other brutes have none:
Rhinoceros, you *are* an ugly beast.

HILAIRE BELLOC

THE WILLOW CATS

They call them pussy-willows,
    But there's no cat to see
Except the little furry toes
    That stick out on the tree:

I think that very long ago,
    When I was just born new,
There must have been whole pussy-cats
    Where just the toes stick through—

And every Spring it worries me,
    I cannot ever find
Those willow-cats that ran away
    And left their toes behind!

               MARGARET WIDDEMER

CATS

"Pussy-cat, pussy-cat, where have you been?"
"I have been up to London to look at the Queen."
"Pussy-cat, pussy-cat, what did you there?"
"I frightened a little mouse under the chair."

231

"Hie, hic," says Anthony,
"Puss in the pantry,
Gnawing, gnawing
A mutton mutton-bone;
See how she tumbles it,
See how she mumbles it,
See how she tosses
The mutton mutton-bone."

I love little pussy, her coat is so warm;
And if I don't hurt her she'll do me no harm.
So I'll not pull her tail nor drive her away,
But pussy and I very gently will play.

Pussy-cat sits by the fire.
    How did she come there?
In walks the little dog,
    Says, "Where is Pussy, where?"

"How d'ye do, Mistress Pussy?
    Mistress Pussy, how d'ye do?"
"I thank you kindly, little dog,
    I fare as well as you."

OLD RHYMES

A KITTEN'S THOUGHT

It's very nice to think of how
In every country lives a Cow
To furnish milk with all her might
For Kitten's comfort and delight.

OLIVER HERFORD

THE KITTEN SPEAKS

I am the Cat of Cats. I am
   The everlasting cat!
Cunning, and old, and sleek as jam,
   The everlasting cat!
I hunt the vermin in the night—
   The everlasting cat!
For I see best without the light—
   The everlasting cat!

WILLIAM BRIGHTY RANDS

THEN THEY BEGAN TO CRY

THE CARELESS KITTENS

Three little kittens
They lost their mittens;
   Then they began to cry
      Miaow! Miaow! Miaow!
"Oh, mother dear,
We greatly fear
   Our mittens we have lost!
      Miaow! Miaow! Miaow!"
"What! lost your mittens!
You naughty kittens!
   Now you shall have no pie!
      Miaow! Miaow! Miaow!"

Three little kittens
They searched for mittens,
   Then they began to cry:
      Miaow! Miaow! Miaow!
"Oh, mother dear,
See here! See here!
   Our mittens we have found!
      Miaow! Miaow! Miaow!"
"What! found your mittens!
You darling kittens!
   Now you shall have some pie!
      Miaow! Miaow! Miaow! Miaow! Miaow! Miaow!"

                    OLD RHYME

"OH, MOTHER DEAR, SEE HERE! SEE HERE!"

THE RESOLUTE CAT

A gray cat, very willful, took a notion once to wander
  And clawing (and pawing), climbed up into a tree.
"I'll hide here and bide here, and have a nap beside here,
  And I won't come down for a kingdom, indeed I won't," said he.

But a small girl, very lonely, kept calling, "Kitty! Kitty!"
  And fearing (and peering), climbed slowly up the tree.
"Oho, sir, I know, sir, you want to stay and doze, sir,
  But won't you change your mind, please, and come on down?" said she.

The gray cat, very scornful, pretended he was snoring.
  "I wouldn't come down for a kingdom, I wouldn't indeed," snored he.
"Oh, gray cat, come away, cat; there's a cream and curds and whey, cat,
  In a blue bowl in the kitchen. And the dog has seen it," said she.

The gray cat, very drowsy, twitched his whiskers, twitched them quickly;
  His big eyes opened, opened, as green as green could be.
"I seem, girl, in a dream, girl, to catch the scent of cream, girl;
  I've napped enough for one day, perhaps I have," said he.

           And, zip! he was out of the tree.
           "Oho, oho!" said she.

                      NANCY BYRD TURNER

THE WHITE CAT AND THE STUDENT[1]

    I and Pangur Bán, my cat,
    'Tis a like task we are at;
    Hunting mice is his delight,
    Hunting words I sit all night.

[1] This poem was originally written in Old Gaelic over a thousand years ago. It was found on the margin of a holy book and was the work of an Irish student; it was made into English some years ago by an English poet. The word *Bán* means "white."

237

Better far than praise of men
'Tis to sit with book and pen;
Pangur bears me no ill-will,
He, too, plies his simple skill.

'Tis a merry thing to see
At our tasks how glad are we,
When at home we sit and find
Entertainment to our mind.

Oftentimes a mouse will stray
In the hero Pangur's way;
Oftentimes my keen thought set
Takes a meaning in its net.

'Gainst the wall he sets his eye
Full and fierce and sharp and sly;
'Gainst the wall of knowledge I
All my little wisdom try.

When a mouse darts from its den,
O! how glad is Pangur then;
O! what gladness do I prove
When I solve the doubts I love.

So in peace our task we ply,
Pangur Bán, my cat, and I;
In our arts we find our bliss,
I have mine, and he has his.

Practice every day has made
Pangur perfect in his trade;
I get wisdom day and night,
Turning darkness into light.

Adapted from the Irish by
ROBIN FLOWER

THE WILD HOME-PUSSY

I love little pussy, her coat is so warm,
But when she grows vocal she loses her charm.
Her sphere is not the concert stage;
She should know better at her age.

Our very nicest cats don't roam;
A pussy's place is in the home
Purring, and being there to pat.
She should confine herself to that;
Never competing for the honors
Bestowed on human prima donnas.

EMMA ROUNDS

THE OLD DOG

The old dog barks backward without looking up.
I can remember when he was a pup.

ROBERT FROST

ELEGY ON THE DEATH OF A MAD DOG

Good people all, of every sort
  Give ear unto my song;
And if you find it wondrous short,
  It cannot hold you long.

In Islington there was a man,
  Of whom the world might say,
That still a godly race he ran
  Whene'er he went to pray.

239

A kind and gentle heart he had,
    To comfort friends and foes;
The naked every day he clad,
    When he put on his clothes.

And in that town a dog was found,
    As many dogs there be,
Both mongrel, puppy, whelp, and hound,
    And curs of low degree.

This dog and man at first were friends;
    But when a pique [1] began,
The dog, to gain his private ends,
    Went mad, and bit the man.

Around from all the neighboring streets
    The wondering neighbors ran,
And swore the dog had lost his wits,
    To bite so good a man.

The wound it seemed both sore and sad
    To every Christian eye:
And while they swore the dog was mad,
    They swore the man would die.

But soon a wonder came to light,
    That showed the rogues they lied,
The man recovered of the bite,
    The dog it was that died.

OLIVER GOLDSMITH

[1] A feud.

THE LITTLE DOG

(*A Child's Dream*)

I had a little dog, and my dog was very small;
He licked me in the face, and he answered to my call;
Of all the treasures that were mine, I loved him most of all.

His nose was fresh as morning dew and blacker than the night;
I thought that it could even snuff the shadows and the light;
And his tail he held bravely, like a banner in a fight.

His body covered thick with hair was very good to smell;
His little stomach underneath was pink as any shell;
And I loved him and honored him, more than words can tell.

We ran out in the morning, both of us, to play,
Up and down across the fields for all the sunny day;
But he ran so swiftly—he ran right away.

I looked for him, I called him, entreatingly. Alas,
The dandelions could not speak, though they had seen him pass,
And nowhere was his waving tail among the waving grass.

I called him in a thousand ways and yet he did not come;
The pathways and the hedges were horrible and dumb.
I prayed to God who never heard. My desperate soul grew numb.

The sun sank low. I ran; I prayed: "If God has not the power
To find him, let me die. I cannot bear another hour."
When suddenly I came upon a great yellow flower.

And all among its petals, such was Heaven's grace,
In that golden hour, in that golden place,
All among its petals, was his hairy face.

FRANCES CORNFORD

THE DOG

(*As seen by the Cat*)

The Dog is black or white or brown,
    And sometimes spotted like a clown.
He loves to make a foolish noise,
    And Human Company enjoys.

The Human People pat his head
    And teach him to pretend he's dead,
And beg, and fetch, and carry, too;
    Things that no well-bred Cat will do.

At Human jokes, however stale,
    He jumps about and wags his tail,
And Human People clap their hands
    And think he really understands.

They say "Good Dog" to him. To us
    They say "Poor Puss," and make no fuss.
Why Dogs are "good" and Cats are "poor"
    I fail to understand, I'm sure."

To Someone very Good and Just,
    Who has proved worthy of her trust,
A Cat will *sometimes* condescend—
    The Dog is Everybody's friend!

OLIVER HERFORD

SONG OF THE RABBITS OUTSIDE A TAVERN

We who play under the pines,
We who dance in the snow
That shines blue in the light of the moon
Sometimes halt as we go,
Stand with our ears erect,
Our noses testing the air
To gaze at the golden world
Behind the windows there.

Suns they have in a cave,
And stars each on a tall white stem,
And the thought of fox or of owl
Seems never to trouble them.
They laugh and eat and are warm,
Their food is ready at hand
While hungry out in the cold
We little rabbits stand.

But they never dance as we dance,
They have not the speed nor the grace,
We scorn both the cat and the dog
Who lie by their fireplace,
We scorn them, licking their paws
Their eyes on an upraised spoon—
We who dance hungry and wild
Under a winter's moon!

ELIZABETH COATSWORTH

THE MOUSE

I heard a mouse
Bitterly complaining
In a crack of moonlight
Aslant on the floor—

"Little I ask
And that little is not granted.
There are few crumbs
In this world any more.

"The bread-box is tin
And I cannot get in.

"The jam's in a jar
My teeth cannot mar.

"The cheese sits by itself
On the pantry shelf—

"All night I run
Searching and seeking,
All night I run
About on the floor,

"Moonlight is there
And a bare place for dancing,
But no little feast
Is spread any more."

ELIZABETH COATSWORTH

SONG OF THE CAMELS

(*Twelfth Night*)

Not born to the forest are we,
Not born to the plain,
To the grass and the shadowing tree
And the splashing of rain.
Only the sand we know
And the cloudless sky,
The mirage and the deep-sunk well
And the stars on high.

To the sound of our bells we came
With huge soft stride,
Kings riding upon our backs,
Slaves at our side.
Out of the east drawn on
By a dream and a star,
Seeking the hills and the groves
Where the fixed towns are.

Our goal was no palace-gate,
No temple of old,
But a child in his mother's lap
In the cloudy cold.
The olives were windy and white,
Dust swirled through the town,
As all in their royal robes
Our masters knelt down.

Then back to the desert we paced
In our phantom state,
And faded again in the sands
That are secret as fate—
Portents of glory and danger
Our dark shadows lay
At the feet of the babe in the manger
And then drifted away.

ELIZABETH COATSWORTH

THE LAMB

Little Lamb, who made thee?
Dost thou know who made thee?
Gave thee life and bid thee feed
By the stream and o'er the mead;
Gave thee clothing of delight,
Softest clothing, woolly, bright;
Gave thee such a tender voice
Making all the vales rejoice?
Little Lamb, who made thee?
Dost thou know who made thee?

Little Lamb, I'll tell thee,
Little Lamb, I'll tell thee:
He is callèd by thy name,
For he calls himself a Lamb.
He is meek and he is mild;
He became a little child.
I a child and thou a lamb,
We are callèd by his name.
Little Lamb, God bless thee.
Little Lamb, God bless thee.

WILLIAM BLAKE

MARY'S LAMB

Mary had a little lamb,
    Its fleece was white as snow;
And everywhere that Mary went,
    The lamb was sure to go.

He followed her to school one day,
    Which was against the rule;
It made the children laugh and play
    To see a lamb at school.

And so the teacher turned him out,
    But still he lingered near,
And waited patiently about
    Till Mary did appear.

Then he ran to her, and he laid
    His head upon her arm,
As if he said, "I'm not afraid—
    You'll keep me from all harm."

"What makes the lamb love Mary so?"
    The eager children cried.
"Oh, Mary loves the lamb, you know,"
    The teacher quick replied.

And you each gentle animal
    In confidence may bind,
And make them follow at your will,
    If you are only kind.

               SARAH JOSEPHA HALE

THE SQUIRREL

Whisky frisky,
Hippety hop,
Up he goes
To the tree top!

Whirly, twirly,
Round and round,
Down he scampers
To the ground.

Furly, curly,
What a tail,
Tall as a feather,
Broad as a sail.

Where's his supper?
In the shell.
Snappy, cracky,
Out it fell.

THE SECRET[1]

A fuzzy fellow without feet
Yet doth exceeding run!
Of velvet is his countenance
And his complexion dun.

Sometimes he dwelleth in the grass,
Sometimes upon a bough
From which he doth descend in plush
Upon the passer-by.

[1] For a humorous version of this poem look on page 444.

All this in summer—but when winds
Alarm the forest folk,
He taketh damask residence
And struts in sewing silk.

Then, finer than a lady,
Emerges in the spring,
A feather on each shoulder—
You'd scarce accredit him.

By men yclept [1] a caterpillar—
By me— But who am I
To tell the .pretty secret
Of the butterfly!

EMILY DICKINSON

THE CATERPILLAR

Brown and furry
Caterpillar, in a hurry
Take your walk
To the shady leaf or stalk
Or what not,
Which may be the chosen spot.
No toad spy you,
Hovering bird of prey pass by you;
Spin and die,
To live again a butterfly.

CHRISTINA ROSSETTI

[1] called.

249

TO A DEAD CRICKET

Never again, beneath some fern or flower,
    Will you lift up a cheerful heart and sing;
Never will I, within some leafy bower,
    Hear the bright music of your golden wing.
        Adapted from MANSALCAS *by* L. U.

THE FLY

    Baby bye,
    Here's a fly,
Let us watch him, you and I.

    How he crawls
    Up the walls,
Yet he never falls.

    There he goes
    On his toes,
Tickling baby's nose.

If you and I had two such legs,
You and I could walk on eggs.

THE PLAYFUL CRICKETS

A grasshopper once had a game of tag
    With some crickets that lived near by,
When he stubbed his toe, and over he went
    Too quick to see with your eye.

Then the crickets leaned up against a tree
   And chirped till their sides were sore;
But the grasshopper said, "You are laughing at me,
   And I won't play any more."

So off he went, though he wanted to stay,
   For he was not hurt by the fall;
And the gay little crickets went on with their play,
   And never missed him at all.

UNKNOWN

THE SPIDER

How doth the jolly little spider
Wind up such miles of silk inside her?
The explanation seems to be
She does not eat so much as me.

And if I never, never cram
Myself with ginger-bread and jam,
Then maybe I'll have room to hide
A little rope in *my* inside.

Then I shall tie it very tight
Just over the electric light,
And hang head downward from the ceiling—
I wonder if one *minds* the feeling?

Or else I'd tie it to a tree
And let myself into the sea;
But when I wound it up again
I wonder if I'd have a pain?

A. P. HERBERT

BEES BEFORE WINTER

His bees went very far that night,
As far as they could go.
Some came back bearing honey;
Some brought flakes of snow!

MERRILL MOORE

LADY-BUG

Lady-bug, lady-bug,
    Fly away home,
Your house is on fire,
    Your children will burn.
All but one
    And her name is Ann,
And she crept under
    The frying-pan.

THE OYSTER

The herring loves the merry moonlight,
    The mackerel loves the wind;
But the oyster loves the deep blue sea,
    For she comes of a gentle kind.

THE TOAD AND THE FROG

"Croak!" said the Toad, "I'm hungry, I think;
Today I've had nothing to eat or to drink;
I'll crawl to a garden and jump through the pales,
And there I'll dine nicely on slugs and on snails."

"Ho, ho!" quoth the Frog, "is that what you mean?
Then I'll hop away to the next meadow stream;
There I will drink, and eat worms and slugs, too,
And then I shall have a good dinner like you."

THE TORTOISE

Safe in his fortress
Of black and gold,
When the world was young
The tortoise was old.

Cabbage and lettuce
Tender and green,
The tortoise changed
To armor clean.

Before King Richard
Was on the throne
He built for his body
A palace of bone.

King Richard is gone:
But safe and still
The tortoise peeps out
From his horny sill.

HERBERT ASQUITH

253

THE BARNACLE

Old Bill Barnacle sticks to his ship,
He never is ill on the stormiest trip;
Upside down he crosses the ocean—
If you do that you *enjoy* the motion.

Barnacle's family grows and grows,
Little relations arrive in rows;
And the quicker the barnacles grow, you know,
The slower the ship doth go—yo, ho!

Thousands of barnacles, small and great,
Stick to the jolly old ship of State;
So we mustn't be cross if she seems to crawl—
It's rather a marvel she goes at all.

A. P. HERBERT

DOLPHINS

The people waddle on the boat
And twaddle on the land,
They boggle everything they note
But cannot understand.

The Dolphins play with spriddle-spray
And tag each other's tail;
The smallest papoose-porpoise
Expects to be a whale.

The people think of everything,
Of gooberbees and eggs,
Of clubs and frills and butcher-bills,
And scarcely move their legs.

But Dolphins never think a wink
Not even in their sleep,
They put sea-polish on their backs,
And leap and *leap* and LEAP!

MOLLY MICHAELS

MINNOWS

. . . Swarms of minnows show their little heads,
Staying their wavy bodies 'gainst the streams,
To taste the luxury of sunny beams
Tempered with coolness. How they ever wrestle
With their own sweet delight, and ever nestle
Their silver bellies on the pebbly sand.
If you but scantily hold out the hand,
That very instant not one will remain;
But turn your eye, and they are there again.
The ripples seem right glad to reach those cresses,
And cool themselves among the em'rald tresses;
The while they cool themselves, they freshness give,
And moisture, that the bowery green may live.

JOHN KEATS

FISHES

From "Kensington Gardens"

Three fishermen
fished in the old Round Pond.
One fished
for fishes of Trebizond—

Golden fishes
with open mouth
stuffed with spice out of
the East and the South.

(He caught nothing)
The second fished
for the sort of whale
in which Jonah swished

through the pale green seas
of the Bible—flup!
before Jonah was ready
he'd coughed him up.

(He caught nothing)
The third with string
hopefully fished
for anything.

Like flourishes made
with a thick-nibbed pen,
the minnows swam up
and swam off again.

And would it surprise you
to learn that the three
ridiculous fishermen
all were me?

HUMBERT WOLFE

MORNING AT THE BEACH

There's soap-suds on the waves,
There's white foam in the sky,
The pebbles on the beach are wet,
And so am I.

There are fishes in the sea,
How many do you think?
How many shining fishes
And do they drink?

If fishes do drink water—
Some day, perhaps, they'll try
To drink

    and drink

        and drink

            *and
drink*

The ocean *dry!*

JOHN FARRAR

THE LOBSTER QUADRILLE

From "Alice in Wonderland"

"Will you walk a little faster?" said a whiting to a snail,
"There's a porpoise close behind us, and he's treading on my tail.
See how eagerly the lobsters and the turtles all advance!
They are waiting on the shingle—will you come and join the dance?
   Will you, won't you, will you, won't you, will you join the dance?
   Will you, won't you, will you, won't you, will you join the dance?

"You can really have no notion how delightful it will be
When they take us up and throw us, with the lobsters out to sea!"
But the snail replied, "Too far, too far!" and gave a look askance—
Said he thanked the whiting kindly, but he would not join the dance.
   Would not, could not, would not, could not, would not join the dance.
   Would not, could not, would not, could not, could not join the dance.

"What matters it how far we go?" his scaly friend replied.
"The further off from England the nearer is to France.
There is another shore, you know, upon the other side.
Then turn not pale, beloved snail, but come and join the dance.
   Will you, won't you, will you, won't you, will you join the dance?
   Will you, won't you, will you, won't you, will you join the dance?"

LEWIS CARROLL

SERIOUS OMISSION

I know that there are dragons,
St. George's, Jason's, too,
And many modern dragons
With scales of green and blue;

But though I've been there many times
And carefully looked through,
I cannot find a dragon
In the cages at the Zoo!

JOHN FARRAR

MIXED BEASTS

The Octopussycat

I love Octopussy, his arms are so long;
There's nothing in nature so sweet as his song.
'Tis true I'd not touch him—no, not for a farm!
If I keep at a distance he'll do me no harm.

The Kangarooster

His tail is remarkably long
And his legs are remarkably strong;
But the strength and the length of his legs and his tail
Are as naught to the strength of his song.

He picks up his food with his bill;
He bounds over valley and hill;
But the height of his bounds can't compare with the sounds
He lets out when he crows with a will.

259

The Herringdove

The gentle, soft-voiced herringdove
    Swims in the sea so wide.
Emblem of innocence and love;
    It's very nice when dried.

The Rhinocerostrich

He surely is not built for speed;
    I don't, myself, think him a beauty;
His strongest traits are wrath and greed;
    Yet, I suppose, he does his duty.

The Bumblebeaver

A cheerful and industrious beast,
    He's always humming as he goes
To make mud-houses with his tail
    Or gather honey with his nose.

Although he flits from flower to flower,
    He's not at all a gay deceiver.
We might take lessons by the hour
    From busy, buzzy Bumblebeaver.

KENYON COX

"I'LL TELL YOU A STORY"

"I'LL TELL YOU A STORY"

Some of these stories are true; others are only poems—but they are true poems.

Two of these stories belong to history. "Barbara Frietchie" was an old lady of ninety when Stonewall Jackson invaded her town during the War between the States, and the poem reflects just as much glory on him as it does on her. "The Pied Piper of Hamelin" is built around a place and legend. The town is a real town—Hamelin is in Germany—and people from all over the world have gone there because of this poem. Whether the legend is true or not is something no one can say for certain. I'm sure I can't. But I do know that there have been many legends about animals who were drawn by the spell of music. All the wild things of the forest came (so they say) when Pan played on his enchanted pipes; and the story of Orpheus tells that when he struck the lyre (an instrument given to him by the god Apollo) he was followed about not only by wild beasts and birds, but by trees and rocks which tore themselves up to follow the sound of his golden harp. Even today, snake-charmers in India train poisonous cobras to do their bidding by playing on flutes. So it isn't hard for me to believe that an expert piper (who seems also to have been something of a magician) may have charmed the rats away. But there's no reason why *you* have to believe it, even though Hamelin has just celebrated the five hundred and sixtieth anniversary of this great event.

About some of the other stories: "The Babes in the Wood" is one of the oldest. Perhaps you have read a version of it in your book of fairy tales, and part of it is like the opera "Hänsel and Gretel." You can see how it turned into a much longer poem in "The Ingoldsby Legends" or a more humorous one in Guy Wetmore Carryl's clever "How the Babes in the Wood Showed They Couldn't Be Beaten" on page 344. "Meg Merrilies" is the story of an old gypsy woman—really it's more a picture than a story—by John Keats, one of the greatest poets who ever lived. "The Three Beggars" is a poem of pure magic, of how three poor men were rewarded by a miracle. "As Lucy Went A-Walking," written by the same man who wrote "The Three Beggars" (do you remember his delightful "Jim Jay" on page 139), is a poem about witch-craft, and you don't have to believe this one either if you don't care to.

Countless are the stories about the frog who would a-wooing go. I've placed two of them together here—one of the oldest English versions and one from the Kentucky Mountains where I heard it sung to the notes of a country fiddle. The Kentucky Mountains also gave us "The Swapping Song" which was sung, somewhat differently, in England before Kentucky ever saw a white man. "The Lady and the Swine," "The Queer Ship" and "A Strange Story" are still older, and sometimes appear among the nursery rhymes.

Perhaps you all know "A Visit from St. Nicholas," and perhaps some of you will turn up your noses at seeing so familiar a poem in print again. But it's just possible that there are a few children today who don't know the favorite of my childhood. Besides, I couldn't bear to leave it out. "The Doll's Wooing" and "Little John Bottlejohn" are other story-poems on which I grew up. And it suddenly strikes me that most of the poems I liked best were about rather unlikely things: Landsmen who were flattered—flattered to death—by fish-tailed ladies who lived at the bottom of the sea; and dolls that came to life in the toy-box; and fiddlers who made everything, even the waters, dance whenever they played; and fat Kris Kringles who managed to slide down the narrowest of chimneys.

Then there is the story of the deacon's masterpiece, "The Wonderful One-Hoss Shay," which went to pieces all at once—

> All at once and nothing first,
> Just as bubbles do when they burst.

And then there is . . . But I think I will let you find the others yourself.

THE BABES IN THE WOOD [1]

My dear, do you know
How, a long time ago,
   Two poor little children,
Whose names I don't know,
Were stolen away
On a fine summer's day,
   And left in a wood,
As I've heard people say?

And when it was night,
So sad was their plight,
   The sun it went down,
And the moon gave no light!
They sobbed and they sighed,
And they bitterly cried,
   And the poor little things
They lay down and died.

And when they were dead,
The robins so red
   Brought strawberry leaves
And over them spread;
And all the day long
They sang them this song:
"Poor babes in the wood!
Poor babes in the wood!
   And don't you remember
The babes in the wood?"

OLD BALLAD

[1] A humorous treatment of this old tale is on page 344.

TIGGADY RUE

Curious, curious Tiggady Rue
Looks and looks in the heart of you;
She finds you good,
She finds you bad,
Generous, mean,
Grumpy, glad—
Tiggady Rue.

Curious, curious Tiggady Rue
Tells your thoughts and tells you *you*:
Elephant thoughts,
And spry and lean,
And thoughts made like a jumping bean;
Or wedgy ones
Slid in between—
She knows them, too,
If she looks at you,
Tiggady Rue.

Curious, curious Tiggady Rue
Knows' your thoughts, and you, and you;
When dusk is down
On field and town,
Beware!
Take care!
If she looks at you—
Tiggady Rue.

DAVID MC CORD

BARBARA FRIETCHIE

Up from the meadows rich with corn,
Clear in the cool September morn,

The clustered spires of Frederick stand
Green-walled by the hills of Maryland.

Round about them orchards sweep,
Apple and peach tree fruited deep,

Fair as the garden of the Lord
To the eyes of the famished rebel horde,

On that pleasant morn of the early fall
When Lee marched over the mountain-wall;

Over the mountains winding down,
Horse and foot, into Frederick town.

Forty flags with their silver stars,
Forty flags with their crimson bars,

Flapped in the morning wind: the sun
Of noon looked down, and saw not one.

Up rose old Barbara Frietchie then,
Bowed with her fourscore years and ten;

Bravest of all in Frederick town,
She took up the flag the men hauled down;

In her attic window the staff she set,
To show that one heart was loyal yet.

Up the street came the rebel tread,
Stonewall Jackson riding ahead.

Under his slouched hat left and right
He glanced; the old flag met his sight.

"Halt!"—the dust-brown ranks stood fast.
"Fire!"—out blazed the rifle-blast.

It shivered the window, pane and sash;
It rent the banner with seam and gash.

Quick, as it fell, from the broken staff
Dame Barbara snatched the silken scarf.

She leaned far out on the window-sill,
And shook it forth with a royal will.

"Shoot, if you must, this old gray head,
But spare your country's flag," she said.

A shade of sadness, a blush of shame,
Over the face of the leader came;

The nobler nature within him stirred
To life at that woman's deed and word;

"Who touches a hair of yon gray head
Dies like a dog! March on!" he said.

All day long through Frederick street
Sounded the tread of marching feet:

All day long that free flag tossed
Over the heads of the rebel host.

Ever its torn folds rose and fell
On the loyal winds that loved it well;

And through the hill-gaps sunset light
Shone over it with a warm good-night.

Barbara Frietchie's work is o'er,
And the Rebel rides on his raids no more.

Honor to her! and let a tear
Fall, for her sake, on Stonewall's bier.

Over Barbara Frietchie's grave,
Flag of Freedom and Union, wave!

Peace and order and beauty draw
Round thy symbol of light and law;

And ever the stars above look down
On thy stars below in Frederick town!

JOHN GREENLEAF WHITTIER

THE PIED PIPER OF HAMELIN

I

Hamelin town's in Brunswick,
  By famous Hanover city;
The River Weser, deep and wide,
Washes its walls on the southern side;
A pleasanter spot you never spied;
  But, when begins my ditty,
Almost five hundred years ago,
To see the townsfolk suffer so
  From vermin, was a pity.

II

  Rats!
They fought the dogs and killed the cats,
  And bit the babies in the cradles,
And ate the cheeses out of the vats,
  And licked the soup from the cooks' own ladles,
Split open the kegs of salted sprats,
Made nests inside men's Sunday hats,
And even spoiled the women's chats,
  By drowning their speaking
  With shrieking and squeaking
In fifty different sharps and flats.

III

At last the people in a body
  To the Town Hall came flocking:
" 'Tis clear," cried they, "our Mayor's a noddy,
  "And as for our Corporation—shocking
"To think we buy gowns lined with ermine
"For dolts that can't or won't determine
"What's best to rid us of our vermin!
"You hope, because you're old and obese,
"To find in the furry civic robe ease!
"Rouse up, Sirs! Give your brains a racking
"To find the remedy we're lacking,
"Or, sure as fate, we'll send you packing!"
At this the Mayor and Corporation
Quaked with a mighty consternation.

IV

An hour they sate in Council;
At length the Mayor broke silence:
"For a guilder I'd my ermine gown sell;
"I wish I were a mile hence!
"It's easy to bid one rack one's brain—
"I'm sure my poor head aches again,
"I've scratched it so, and all in vain.
"Oh, for a trap, a trap, a trap!"
Just as he said this, what should hap
At the chamber door, but a gentle tap.
"Bless us!" cried the Mayor, "what's that?"
(With the Corporation as he sat,
Looking little though wondrous fat;

271

Nor brighter was his eye, nor moister
Than a too-long-opened oyster,
Save when at noon his paunch grew mutinous
For a plate of turtle green and glutinous.)
"Only a scraping of shoes on the mat!
"Anything like the sound of a rat
"Makes my heart go pit-a-pat!"

V

"Come in!" the Mayor cried, looking bigger,
And in did come the strangest figure!
His queer long coat, from heel to head
Was half of yellow and half of red;
And he himself was tall and thin,
With sharp blue eyes, each like a pin,
And light loose hair, yet swarthy skin;
No tuft on cheek nor beard on chin,
But lips where smiles went out and in;
There was no guessing his kith and kin;
And nobody could enough admire
The tall man and his quaint attire.
Quoth one: "It's as if my great-grandsire,
"Starting up at the trump of Doom's tone,
"Had walked this way from his painted tombstone!"

VI

He advanced to the council table:
And, "Please your honors," said he, "I'm able,
"By means of a secret charm, to draw
"All creatures living beneath the sun,
"That creep, or swim, or fly, or run,
"After me so as you never saw!

HE ADVANCED TO THE COUNCIL TABLE

"And I chiefly use my charm
"On creatures that do people harm,—
"The mole, the toad, the newt, the viper:
"And people call me the Pied Piper."
(And here they noticed round his neck
A scarf of red and yellow stripe
To match his coat of the self-same check;
And at the scarf's end hung a pipe;
And his fingers, they noticed, were ever straying
As if impatient to be playing
Upon his pipe, as low it dangled
Over his vesture so old-fangled.)
"Yet," said he, "poor piper as I am,
"In Tartary I freed the Cham,
"Last June, from his huge swarm of gnats;
"I eased in Asia the Nizam
"Of a monstrous brood of vampire bats:
"And as for what your brain bewilders,
"If I can rid your town of rats
"Will you give me a thousand guilders?"
"One! fifty thousand!" was the exclamation
Of the astonished Mayor and Corporation.

VII

Into the street the Piper stept,
　　Smiling first a little smile,
As if he knew what magic slept
　　In his quiet pipe the while;
Then, like a musical adept,
To blow the pipe his lips he wrinkled,
And green and blue his sharp eyes twinkled,
Like a candle-flame where salt is sprinkled;

And ere three shrill notes the pipe had uttered,
You heard as if an army muttered;
And the muttering grew to a grumbling;
And the grumbling grew to a mighty rumbling;
And out of the houses the rats came tumbling.
Great rats, small rats, lean rats, brawny rats,
Brown rats, black rats, gray rats, tawny rats,
Grave old plodders, gay young friskers,
    Fathers, mothers, uncles, cousins,
Cocking tails, and pricking whiskers,
    Families by tens and dozens,
Brothers, sisters, husbands, wives—
Followed the Piper for their lives.

From street to street he piped, advancing,
And step for step they followed dancing,
Until they came to the River Weser,
Wherein all plunged and perished!
—Save one, who, stout as Julius Caesar,
Swam across and lived to carry
(As he, the manuscript he cherished)
To Rat-land home his commentary:
Which was, "At the first shrill note of the pipe
"I heard a sound as of scraping tripe,
"And putting apples, wondrous ripe,
"Into a cider-press's gripe:
"And a moving away of pickle-tub boards,
"And a leaving ajar of conserve-cupboards,
"And a drawing the corks of train-oil-flasks,
"And a breaking the hoops of butter-casks:
"And it seemed as if a voice
"(Sweeter far than by harp or by psaltery
"Is breathed) called out, 'Oh, rats, rejoice!
" 'The world is grown to one vast drysaltery!
" 'So munch on, crunch on, take your nuncheon,
" 'Breakfast, dinner, supper, luncheon!'
"And just as a bulky sugar-puncheon,
"All ready staved, like a great sun shone
"Glorious, scarce an inch before me,
"Just as methought it said, 'Come, bore me!'
"—I found the Weser rolling o'er me."

VIII

You should have heard the Hamelin people
Ringing the bells till they rocked the steeple.
"Go," cried the Mayor, "and get long poles,
"Poke out the nests, and block up the holes!

"Consult with carpenters and builders,
"And leave in our town not even a trace
"Of the rats!" When suddenly, up the face
Of the Piper perked in the market-place,
With a, "First, if you please, my thousand guilders!"

IX

A thousand guilders! The Mayor looked blue;
So did the Corporation, too.
For Council dinners made rare havoc
With Claret, Moselle, Vin-de-Grave, Hock; [1]
And half the money would replenish
Their cellar's biggest butt with Rhenish.
To pay this sum to a wandering fellow,
With a gypsy coat of red and yellow!
"Beside," quoth the Mayor, with a knowing wink,
"Our business was done at the river's brink;
"We saw with our eyes the vermin sink,
"And what's dead can't come to life, I think.
"So, friend, we're not the folks to shrink
"From the duty of giving you something to drink,
"And a matter of money to put in your poke;
"But, as for the guilders, what we spoke
"Of them, as you very well know, was in joke.
"Beside, our losses have made us thrifty.
"A thousand guilders! Come, take fifty!"

X

The Piper's face fell, and he cried,
"No trifling! I can't wait, beside!

[1] These are all names of French and German wines.

"I've promised to visit by dinner-time
"Bagdad, and accept the prime
"Of the Head-Cook's pottage, all he's rich in,
"For having left, in the Caliph's kitchen,
"Of a nest of scorpions no survivor.
"With him I proved no bargain-driver;
"With you, don't think I'll bate a stiver!
"And folks who put me in a passion
"May find me pipe after another fashion."

XI

"How!" cried the Mayor, "d'ye think I'll brook
"Being worse treated than a Cook?
"Insulted by a lazy ribald
"With idle pipe and vesture piebald!
"You threaten us, fellow! Do your worst!
"Blow your pipe there till you burst!"

XII

Once more he stept into the street,
    And to his lips again
Laid his long pipe of smooth, straight cane;
    And ere he blew three notes (such sweet
Soft notes as yet musician's cunning
    Never gave the enraptured air)
There was a rustling that seemed like a bustling
Of merry crowds justling at pitching and hustling,
Small feet were pattering, wooden shoes clattering,
Little hands clapping and little tongues chattering,
And, like fowls in a farmyard when barley is scattering,

RAN MERRILY AFTER THE WONDERFUL MUSIC

Out came the children running.
And all the little boys and girls,
With rosy cheeks and flaxen curls,
And sparkling eyes and teeth like pearls,
Tripping and skipping ran merrily after
The wonderful music with shouting and laughter.

XIII

The Mayor was dumb, and the Council stood
As if they were changed into blocks of wood,
Unable to move a step, or cry
To the children merrily skipping by,
—Could only follow with the eye
That joyous crowd at the Piper's back.
And now the Mayor was on the rack,
And the wretched Council's bosoms beat,
As the Piper turned from the High Street
To where the Weser rolled its waters
Right in the way of their sons and daughters!
However he turned from South to West,
And to Koppelberg Hill his steps addressed,
And after him the children pressed;
Great was the joy in every breast.
"He never can cross that mighty top!
"He's forced to let the piping drop,
"And we shall see our children stop!"
When, lo, as they reached the mountain-side,
A wondrous portal opened wide,
As if a cavern was suddenly hollowed;
And the Piper advanced, and the children followed,
And when all were in to the very last,
The door in the mountain-side shut fast.

Did I say all? No! One was lame,
And could not dance the whole of the way;
And in after years, if you would blame
His sadness, he was used to say,—
"It's dull in our town since my playmates left!
"I can't forget that I'm bereft
"Of all the pleasant sights they see,
"Which the Piper also promised me:
"For he led us, he said, to a joyous land,
"Joining the town and just at hand,
"Where waters gushed and fruit trees grew,
"And flowers put forth a fairer hue,
"And everything was strange and new;

"The sparrows were brighter than peacocks here,
"And their dogs outran our fallow-deer,
"And honey-bees had lost their stings,
"And horses were born with eagles' wings:
"And just as I became assured
"My lame foot would be speedily cured,
"The music stopped, and I stood still,
"And found myself outside the hill,
"Left alone against my will,
"To go now limping as before,
"And never hear of that country more!"

XIV

Alas, alas for Hamelin!
    There came into many a burgher's pate
    A text which says that Heaven's gate
    Opes to the rich at as easy rate
As the needle's eye takes a camel in!
The Mayor sent East, West, North, and South,
To offer the Piper, by word of mouth,
    Wherever it was man's lot to find him,
Silver and gold to his heart's content,
If he'd only return the way he went,
    And bring the children behind him.
But when they saw 'twas a lost endeavor,
And Piper and dancers were gone for ever,
They made a decree that lawyers never
    Should think their records dated duly
If, after the day of the month and the year,
These words did not as well appear,
"And so long after what happened here
    "On the Twenty-second of July,
"Thirteen hundred and seventy-six":

And the better in memory to fix
The place of the children's last retreat,
They called it, the Pied Piper's Street—
Where anyone playing on pipe or tabor
Was sure for the future to lose his labor.
Nor suffered they hostelry or tavern
　　To shock with mirth a street so solemn;
But opposite the place of the cavern
　　They wrote the story on a column,
And on the great church-window painted
The same, to make the world acquainted
How their children were stolen away,
And there it stands to this very day.
And I must not omit to say
That in Transylvania there's a tribe
Of alien people that ascribe
The outlandish ways and dress
On which their neighbors lay such stress,
To their fathers and mothers having risen
Out of some subterraneous prison
Into which they were trepanned
Long ago in a mighty band
Out of Hamelin town in Brunswick land,
But how or why, they don't understand.

XV

So, Willy, let you and me be wipers
Of scores out with all men,—especially pipers!
And, whether they pipe us free from rats or from mice,
If we've promised them aught, let us keep our promise!

ROBERT BROWNING

MEG MERRILIES

Old Meg she was a Gypsy,
    And lived upon the moors:
Her bed it was the brown heath turf,
    And her house was out of doors.

Her apples were swart blackberries,
    Her currants pods o' broom;
Her wine was dew of the wild white rose,
    Her book a churchyard tomb.

Her brothers were the craggy hills,
    Her sisters larchen trees—
Alone with her great family
    She lived as she did please.

No breakfast had she many a morn,
    No dinner many a noon,
And 'stead of supper she would stare
    Full hard against the moon.

But every morn of woodbine fresh
    She made her garlanding,
And every night the dark glen yew
    She wove, and she would sing.

And with her fingers old and brown
    She plaited mats o' rushes,
And gave them to the cottagers
    She met among the bushes.

Old Meg was brave as Margaret Queen
  And tall as Amazon:
An old red blanket cloak she wore;
  A chip hat had she on.
God rest her aged bones somewhere—
  She died full long agone!

JOHN KEATS

THE THREE BEGGARS

'Twas autumn daybreak gold and wild,
  While past St. Ann's gray tower they shuffled,
Three beggars spied a fairy-child
  In crimson mantle muffled.

The daybreak lighted up her face
  All pink, and sharp, and emerald-eyed;
She looked on them a little space,
  And shrill as hautboy [1] cried:

"O three tall footsore men of rags
  Which walking this gold morn I see,
What will ye give me from your bags
  For fairy kisses three?"

The first, that was a reddish man,
  Out of his bundle takes a crust:
"La, by the tombstones of St. Ann,
  There's fee, if fee you must!"

The second, that was a chestnut man,
  Out of his bundle draws a bone:
"La, by the belfry of St. Ann,
  And all my breakfast gone!"

---

[1] An instrument, something like a pipe and something like a horn; also called "oboe."

The third, that was a yellow man,
Out of his bundle picks a groat,
"La, by the Angel of St. Ann,
And I must go without."

That changeling, lean and icy-lipped,
Touched crust, and bone, and groat, and lo!
Beneath her finger taper-tipped
The magic all ran through.

Instead of crust a peacock pie,
Instead of bone sweet venison,
Instead of groat a white lily
With seven blooms thereon.

And each fair cup was deep with wine:
Such was the changeling's charity,
The sweet feast was enough for nine,
But not too much for three.

O toothsome meat in jelly froze!
O tender haunch of elfin stag!
O rich the odor that arose!
O plump with scraps each bag!

There, in the daybreak gold and wild,
Each merry-hearted beggar man
Drank deep unto the fairy child,
And blessed the good St. Ann.

WALTER DE LA MARE

AS LUCY WENT A-WALKING

As Lucy went a-walking one morning cold and fine,
There sate three crows upon a bough, and three times three is nine:
Then "O!" said Lucy, in the snow, "it's very plain to see
A witch has been a-walking in the fields in front of me."

Then stept she light and heedfully across the frozen snow,
And plucked a bunch of elder-twigs that near a pool did grow:
And, by and by, she comes to seven shadows in one place
Stretched black by seven poplar-trees against the sun's bright face.

She looks to left, she looks to right, and in the midst she sees
A little pool of water clear and frozen 'neath the trees;
Then down beside its margent in the crusty snow she kneels,
And hears a magic belfry a-ringing with sweet bells.

Clear sang the faint far merry peal, then silence on the air,
And icy-still the frozen pool and poplars standing there:
Then lo! as Lucy turned her head and looked along the snow,
She sees a witch—a witch she sees, come frisking to and fro.

Her scarlet, buckled shoes they clicked, her heels a-twinkling high;
With mistletoe her steeple-hat bobbed as she capered by;
But never a dint, or mark, or print, in the whiteness for to see,
Though danced she high, though danced she fast, though danced she lissomely.

It seemed 'twas diamonds in the air, or little flakes of frost;
It seemed 'twas golden smoke around, or sunbeams lightly tossed;
It seemed an elfin music like to reeds and warblers rose:
"Nay!" Lucy said, "it is the wind that through the branches flows."

Rainbow in the Sky

And as she peeps, and as she peeps, 'tis no more one but three,
And eye of bat, and downy wing of owl within the tree,
And the bells of that sweet belfry a-pealing as before
And now it is not three she sees, and now it is not four—

"Oh! who are ye," sweet Lucy cries, "that in a dreadful ring,
All muffled up in brindled shawls, do caper, frisk, and spring?"
"A witch, and witches, one and nine," they straight to her reply,
And looked upon her narrowly, with green and needle eye.

Then Lucy sees in clouds of gold, green cherry trees up-grow,
And bushes of red roses that bloomed above the snow;
She smells, all faint, the almond-boughs blowing so wild and fair
And doves with milky eyes ascend fluttering in the air.

Clear flowers she sees, like tulip buds, go floating by like birds,
With wavering tips that warbled sweetly strange enchanted words;
And, as with ropes of amethyst, the boughs with lamps were hung,
And clusters of green emeralds like fruit upon them clung.

"O witches nine, ye dreadful nine, O witches seven and three!
Whence come these wondrous things that I this Christmas morning see?"
But straight, as in a clap, when she of Christmas says the word,
Here is the snow, and there the sun, but never bloom nor bird;

Nor warbling flame, nor gleaming rope of amethyst there shows,
Nor bunches of green emeralds, nor belfry, well, and rose,
Nor cloud of gold, nor cherry-tree, nor witch in brindle shawl,
But like a dream that vanishes, so vanished were they all.

When Lucy sees, and only sees three crows upon a bough,
And earthly twigs, and bushes hidden white in driven snow,
Then "O!" said Lucy, "three times three is nine—I plainly see
Some witch has been a-walking in the fields in front of me."

WALTER DE LA MARE

288

A FROG HE WOULD A-WOOING GO

A frog he would a-wooing go,
  Heigho, says Rowley,
Whether his mother would let him or no.
  With a rowley powley, gammon and spinach,
  Heigho, says Anthony Rowley!

So off he set with his opera hat,
  Heigho, says Rowley,
And on the road he met with a rat.
  With a rowley powley, gammon and spinach,
  Heigho, says Anthony Rowley!

"Pray, Mr. Rat, will you go with me,
  Heigho, says Rowley,
Kind Mrs. Mousey for to see?"
  With a rowley powley, gammon and spinach,
  Heigho, says Anthony Rowley!

When they came to the door of Mousey's hall,
  Heigho, says Rowley,
They gave a loud knock and they gave a loud call.
  With a rowley powley, gammon and spinach,
  Heigho, says Anthony Rowley!

"Pray, Mrs. Mouse, are you within?"
  Heigho, says Rowley.
"Oh, yes, kind sirs, I'm sitting to spin."
  With a rowley powley, gammon and spinach,
  Heigho, says Anthony Rowley!

"Pray, Mrs. Mouse, will you give us some beer?
  Heigho, says Rowley,
For Froggy and I are fond of good cheer."
  With a rowley powley, gammon and spinach,
  Heigho, says Anthony Rowley!

"Pray, Mr. Frog, will you give us a song?
  Heigho, says Rowley,
But let it be something that's not very long."
  With a rowley powley, gammon and spinach,
  Heigho, says Anthony Rowley!

"Indeed, Mrs. Mouse," replied the frog,
  Heigho, says Rowley,
"A cold has made me as hoarse as a dog."
  With a rowley powley, gammon and spinach,
  Heigho, says Anthony Rowley!

"Since you have caught cold, Mr. Frog," Mousey said,
  Heigho, says Rowley,
"I'll sing you a song that I have just made."
  With a rowley powley, gammon and spinach,
  Heigho, says Anthony Rowley!

But while they were making a merry din,
  Heigho, says Rowley,
A cat and her kittens came tumbling in.
  With a rowley powley, gammon and spinach,
  Heigho, says Anthony Rowley!

The cat she seized the rat by the crown;
  Heigho, says Rowley,
The kittens they pulled the little mouse down.
  With a rowley powley, gammon and spinach,
  Heigho, says Anthony Rowley!

This put Mr. Frog in a terrible fright,
 Heigho, says Rowley,
He took up his hat, and he wished them good night.
 With a rowley powley, gammon and spinach,
 Heigho, says Anthony Rowley!

But as Froggy was crossing over a brook,
 Heigho, says Rowley,
A lily-white duck came and gobbled him up.
 With a rowley powley, gammon and spinach,
 Heigho, says Anthony Rowley!

So there was an end of one, two, and three,
 Heigho, says Rowley,
The Rat, the Mouse, and the little Frog-gee!
 With a rowley powley, gammon and spinach,
 Heigho, says Anthony Rowley!

OLD ENGLISH SONG

THE FROG'S COURTIN'

Frog went a-courtin' an' he did ride;
  A-hum—
Sword and buckler by his side;
  A-hum.

Across the river he did swim;
  A-hum—
"Pray, Miss Mouse, are you within?"
  A-hum.

He took that lady Mouse on his knee;
  A-hum—
An' says, "Miss Mousie, will you marry me?"
  A-hum.

Says she, "Before I think of that,
    A-hum—
I'll have to ask my Uncle Rat.
    A-hum."

"Not without Uncle Rat's consent,
    A-hum—
Would I marry the President.
    A-hum."

Uncle Rat he went to town,
    A-hum—
To buy his niece a wedding-gown.
    A-hum.

What will the wedding-supper be?
    A-hum—
A fried mosquito an' a black-eyed pea.
    A-hum.

First came in was a bumble-bee,
    A-hum—
Fiddle and bow upon his knee.
    A-hum.

Nex' came in was two little ants,
    A-hum—
Fixin' themselves for to have a dance.
    A-hum.

Nex' came in was a butterfly,
    A-hum—
Passin' the butter on the sly.
    A-hum.

Nex' came in was a garter-snake,
> A-hum—
Curled himself roun' the wedding-cake.
> A-hum.

Nex' came in was a big Tom cat,
> A-hum—
He gobbled the snake an' the mouse an' the rat.
> A-hum.

Frog jumped up and dived in the glen,
> A-hum—
An' nobody ever saw him again.
> Amen!

> KENTUCKY MOUNTAIN SONG

THE SWAPPING SONG

My father he died, but I never knew how.
He left me six horses to drive in my plow.
> With a wim, wam, waddle-o,
> Stick, stock, straddle-o,
> Fin, fan, faddle-o,
> All the way home.

I sold my six horses and bought me a cow
To make me a fortune but I didn't know how.
> With a wim, wam, etc.

I sold my cow and bought me a calf,
And in that trade I lost just half.
> With a wim, wam, etc.

I sold my calf and bought me a mule,
And then I rode like a gol-darned fool.
> With a wim, wam, etc.

293

I sold my mule and swapped it for a pig;
It wouldn't grow much and it wasn't very big.
   With a wim, wam, etc.

I sold my pig and bought me a cat;
The pretty little creature in the corner sat.
   With a wim, wam, etc.

I sold my cat and bought me a mouse;
His tail caught fire and burned down the house.
   With a wim, wam, waddle-o,
   Stick, stock, straddle-o,
   Fin, fan, faddle-o,
   All the way home.

                KENTUCKY MOUNTAIN SONG

THE LADY AND THE SWINE

There was a lady loved a swine:
  "Honey," quoth she,
"Pig-hog, wilt thou be mine?"
  "Grunt," quoth he.

"I'll build thee a silver stye,
    Honey," quoth she;
"And in it thou shalt lie."
    "Grunt," quoth he.

"Pinned with a silver pin,
   Honey," quoth she,
"That you may go out and in."
   "Grunt," quoth he.

"Wilt thou now have me,
Honey?" quoth she.
"Grunt, grunt, grunt," quoth he,
And went his way.

OLD RHYME

THE QUEER SHIP

I saw a ship a-sailing,
   A-sailing on the sea;
And, oh! it was all laden
   With pretty things for thee!

There were comfits in the cabin,
   And apples in the hold
The sails were made of silk,
   And the masts were made of gold.

The four-and-twenty sailors
   That stood between the decks,
Were four-and-twenty white mice
   With chains about their necks.

The captain was a duck,
   With a packet on his back;
And when the ship began to move,
   The captain said, "Quack! Quack!"

                                    OLD RHYME

A STRANGE STORY

There was an old woman, as I've heard tell,
She went to market her eggs to sell;
She went to market all on a market-day,
And she fell asleep on the king's highway.

There came by a peddler whose name was Stout;
He cut her petticoats all round about;

He cut her petticoats up to the knees,
Which made the old woman to shiver and freeze.

When this little woman first did wake,
She began to shiver and she began to shake;
She began to wonder and she began to cry,
"Oh! deary, deary me, this is none of I!

"But if it be I, as I do hope it be,
I've a little dog at home, and he'll know me;
If it be I, he'll wag his little tail,
And if it be not I, he'll loudly bark and wail."

Home went the little woman all in the dark;
Up got the little dog, and he began to bark;
He began to bark, so she began to cry,
"Oh! deary, deary me, this is none of I!"

OLD RHYME

A TRUE STORY

There was a little rabbit sprig,
Who being little, was not big;
He always walked upon his feet,
And never starved when he did eat.
When from a place he ran away,
He never at that place did stay;
And when he ran, as I am told,
He ne'er stood still for young or old.
Though ne'er instructed by a cat,
He knew a mouse was not a rat:
One day, as I am certified,
He took a whim and fairly died;
And, as I'm told by men of sense,
He never has been walking since.

OLD RHYME

300

YESTERDAY IN OXFORD STREET

Yesterday in Oxford Street, oh, what d'you think, my dears?
I had the most exciting time I've had for years and years;
The buildings looked so straight and tall, the sky was blue between,
And, riding on a motor-bus, I saw the fairy queen!

Sitting there upon the rail and bobbing up and down,
The sun was shining on her wings and on her golden crown;
And looking at the shops she was, the pretty silks and lace—
She seemed to think that Oxford Street was quite a lovely place.

And once she turned and looked at me, and waved her little hand;
But I could only stare and stare—oh, would she understand?
I simply couldn't speak at all, I simply couldn't stir,
And all the rest of Oxford Street was just a shining blur.

Then suddenly she shook her wings—a bird had fluttered by—
And down into the Street she looked and up into the sky;
And perching on the railing on a tiny fairy toe,
She flashed away so quickly that I hardly saw her go.

I never saw her any more, altho' I looked all day;
Perhaps she only came to peep, and never meant to stay:
But oh, my dears, just think of it, just think what luck for me,
That she should come to Oxford Street, and I be there to see!

ROSE FYLEMAN

A VISIT FROM ST. NICHOLAS

'Twas the night before Christmas, when all through the house
Not a creature was stirring, not even a mouse;
The stockings were hung by the chimney with care,
In hopes that St. Nicholas soon would be there;
The children were nestled all snug in their beds,
While visions of sugar-plums danced in their heads;
And mamma in her kerchief, and I in my cap,
Had just settled our brains for a long winter nap,—
When out on the lawn there arose such a clatter,
I sprang from my bed to see what was the matter.
Away to the window I flew like a flash,
Tore open the shutters and threw up the sash.
The moon, on the breast of the new-fallen snow,
Gave a luster of midday to objects below;
When what to my wondering eyes should appear
But a miniature sleigh and eight tiny reindeer,
With a little old driver, so lively and quick,
I knew in a moment it must be St. Nick.
More rapid than eagles his coursers they came,
And he whistled, and shouted, and called them by name;
"Now, Dasher! now, Dancer! now, Prancer and Vixen!
On, Comet! On, Cupid! On, Dunder and Blixen!—
To the top of the porch! to the top of the wall!
Now, dash away, dash away, dash away all!"
As dry leaves that before the wild hurricane fly,
When they meet with an obstacle, mount to the sky,
So up to the house-top the coursers they flew,

With the sleigh full of toys—and St. Nicholas, too.
And then in a twinkling I heard on the roof
The prancing and pawing of each little hoof.
As I drew in my head, and was turning around,
Down the chimney St. Nicholas came with a bound.
He was dressed all in fur from his head to his foot,
And his clothes were all tarnished with ashes and soot,
A bundle of toys he had flung on his back,
And he looked like a peddler just opening his pack.
His eyes, how they twinkled! his dimples, how merry!
His cheeks were like roses, his nose like a cherry;
His droll little mouth was drawn up like a bow,
And the beard on his chin was as white as the snow.
The stump of a pipe he held tight in his teeth,
And the smoke, it encircled his head like a wreath.
He had a broad face and a little round belly
That shook, when he laughed, like a bowl full of jelly.
He was chubby and plump—a right jolly old elf;
And I laughed when I saw him, in spite of myself.
A wink of his eye, and a twist of his head,
Soon gave me to know I had nothing to dread.
He spoke not a word, but went straight to his work,
And filled all the stockings; then turned with a jerk,
And laying his finger aside of his nose,
And giving a nod, up the chimney he rose.
He sprang to his sleigh, to his team gave a whistle,
And away they all flew like the down of a thistle;
But I heard him exclaim, ere he drove out of sight,
"Happy Christmas to all, and to all a good-night!"

CLEMENT C. MOORE

THE DOLL'S WOOING

The little French doll was a dear little doll
  Tricked out in the sweetest of dresses;
    Her eyes were of hue
    A most delicate blue
  And dark as the night were her tresses;
Her dear little mouth was fluted and red,
And this little French doll was so very well bred
That whenever accosted her little mouth said:
    "Mamma! mamma!"

The stockinet doll, with one arm and one leg,
  Had once been a handsome young fellow,
    But now he appeared
    Rather frowzy and bleared
  In his torn regimentals of yellow;
Yet his heart gave a curious thump as he lay
In the little toy cart near the window one day
And heard the sweet voice of that French dolly say:
    "Mamma! mamma!"

He listened so long and he listened so hard
  That anon he grew ever so tender,
    For it's everywhere known
    That the feminine tone
  Has a way with all masculine gender!
He up and he wooed her with soldierly zest,
But all she'd reply to the love he professed
Were *these* plaintive words (which perhaps you have guessed):
    "Mamma! mamma!"

Her mother—a sweet little lady of five—
  Vouchsafed her parental protection,
    And although stockinet
    Wasn't blue-blooded, yet

She really could make no objection!
So soldier and dolly were wedded one day,
And a moment ago, as I journeyed that way,
I'm sure that I heard a wee baby voice say:
"Mamma! mamma!"

EUGENE FIELD

LITTLE JOHN BOTTLEJOHN

Little John Bottlejohn lived on the hill,
And a blithe little man was he.
And he won the heart of a pretty mermaid
Who lived in the deep blue sea.
And every evening she used to sit
And sing by the rocks of the sea,
"Oh! little John Bottlejohn, pretty John Bottlejohn,
Won't you come out to me?"

Little John Bottlejohn heard her song,
And he opened his little door.
And he hopped and he skipped, and he skipped and he hopped,
Until he came down to the shore.
And there on the rocks sat the little mermaid,
And still she was singing so free,
"Oh! little John Bottlejohn, pretty John Bottlejohn,
Won't you come out to me?"

Little John Bottlejohn made a bow,
And the mermaid, she made one too;
And she said, "Oh! I never saw anyone half
So perfectly sweet as you!
In my lovely home 'neath the ocean foam,
How happy we both might be!
Oh! little John Bottlejohn, pretty John Bottlejohn,
Won't you come down with me?"

305

Little John Bottlejohn said, "Oh yes!
   I'll willingly go with you.
And I never shall quail at the sight of your tail,
   For perhaps I may grow one, too."
So he took her hand, and he left the land,
   And plunged in the foaming main.
And little John Bottlejohn, pretty John Bottlejohn,
   Never was seen again.

LAURA E. RICHARDS

THE SEVEN FIDDLERS

A blue robe on their shoulders,
   And an ivory bow in hand,
Seven fiddlers came with their fiddles
   A-fiddling through the land,
And they fiddled a tune on their fiddles
   That none could understand.

For none who heard their fiddling
   Might keep his ten toes still,
E'en the cripple threw down his crutches,
   And danced against his will:
Young and old they fell a-dancing,
   While the fiddlers fiddle their fill.

They fiddled down to the ferry—
   The ferry by Severn-side,
And they stept aboard the ferry,
   None else to row or guide,
And deftly steered the pilot,
   And stoutly the oars they plied.

Then suddenly in mid-channel
  These fiddlers ceased to row,
And the pilot spake to his fellows
  In a tongue that none may know:
"Let us home to our fathers and brothers,
  And the maidens we love below."

Then the fiddlers seized their fiddles,
  And sang to their fiddles a song:
"We are coming, coming, oh brothers,
  To the home we have left so long,
For the world still loves the fiddler,
  And the fiddler's tune is strong."

Then they stepped from out the ferry
  Into the Severn-sea,
Down into the depths of the waters
  Where the homes of the fiddlers be,
And the ferry-boat drifted slowly
  Forth to the ocean free!

But where those jolly fiddlers
  Walked down into the deep,
The ripples are never quiet,
  But forever dance and leap,
Though the Severn-sea be silent,
  And the winds be all asleep.

SEBASTIAN EVANS

THE SAILOR GIRL

When the Wild Geese were flying to Flanders away,
I clung to my Desmond beseeching him to stay,
But the stern trumpet sounded the summons to sea,
And afar the ship bore him, *Mabouchal machree*.[1]

[1] My heart's own boy.

And first he sent letters, and then he sent none,
And three times into prison I dreamt he was thrown;
So I cut my long tresses, and stained my face brown,
And went for a sailor from Limerick Town.

Oh! the ropes cut my fingers, but steadfast I strove,
Till I reached the Low Country in search of my love.
There I heard how at Namur his heart was so high,
That they carried him captive, refusing to fly.

With that to King William himself I was brought,
And his mercy for Desmond with tears I besought.
He considered my story, then, smiling, says he,
"The young Irish rebel for your sake is free.

"Bring the varlet before us. Now, Desmond O'Hea,
Myself has decided your sentence today.
You must marry your sailor, with bell, book and ring,
And here is her dowry," cried William the King!

ALFRED PERCIVAL GRAVES

THE OUTLANDISH KNIGHT

An outlandish knight came from the North
   A-wooing with buckler and blade;
And he promised to take her into the North,
   And there he would marry the maid.

"Come fetch me some of your father's gold
   And some of your mother's fee;
And two of the best nags out of the stable,
   Where they stand thirty and three."

She fetched him some of her father's gold
   And some of her mother's fee;
And two of the best nags out of the stable,
   Where they stood thirty and three.

She mounted her on her milk-white steed,
    He on the dapple gray;
They rode till they came unto the sea-side,
    Three hours before it was day.

"Light off, light off thy milk-white steed,
    And deliver it unto me;
Six pretty maids have I drowned here,
    And thou the seventh shall be.

"Pull off, pull off thy silken gown,
    And deliver it unto me,
Methinks it looks too rich and too gay
    To rot in the salt, salt sea.

"Pull off, pull off thy silken stays,
    And deliver them unto me!
Methinks they are too fine and gay
    To rot in the salt, salt sea.

"Pull off, pull off thy Holland smock,
    And deliver it unto me;
Methinks it looks too rich and gay
    To rot in the salt, salt sea."

"If I must pull off my Holland smock,
    Pray turn thy back unto me,
For it is not fitting that such a ruffian
    A woman unclad should see."

He turned his back towards her,
    And looked to the leaf of the tree;
She caught him round the middle so small,
    And tumbled him into the sea.

He dropped high, and he dropped low,
   Until he came to the tide—
"Catch hold of my hand, my pretty maiden,
   And I will make you my bride."

"Lie there, lie there, you false-hearted man,
   Lie there instead of me;
Six pretty maidens have you drowned here,
   And the seventh has drowned thee."

She mounted on her milk-white steed,
   And led the dapple gray,
She rode till she came to her father's hall,
   Three hours before it was day.

OLD BALLAD

PAUL REVERE'S RIDE

Listen, my children, and you shall hear
Of the midnight ride of Paul Revere,
On the eighteenth of April, in seventy-five;
Hardly a man is now alive
Who remembers that famous day and year.
He said to his friend, "If the British march
By land or sea from the town tonight,
Hang a lantern aloft in the belfry arch
Of the North Church tower as a signal light,—
One, if by land, and two, if by sea;
And I on the opposite shore will be,
Ready to ride and spread the alarm
Through every Middlesex village and farm,
For the country folk to be up and to arm."

Then he said, "Good night!" and with muffled oar
Silently rowed to the Charlestown shore,
Just as the moon rose over the bay,
Where swinging wide at her moorings lay
The *Somerset,* British man-of-war;
A phantom ship, with each mast and spar
Across the moon like a prison bar,
And a huge black hulk, that was magnified
By its own reflection in the tide.

Meanwhile, his friend, through alley and street,
Wanders and watches with eager ears,
Till in the silence around him he hears
The muster of men at the barrack door,
The sound of arms, and the tramp of feet,
And the measured tread of the grenadiers,
Marching down to their boats on the shore.

Then he climbed the tower of the Old North Church
By the wooden stairs, with stealthy tread,
To the belfry-chamber overhead,
And startled the pigeons from their perch
On the somber rafters, that round him made
Masses and moving shapes of shade,—
By the trembling ladder, steep and tall,
To the highest window in the wall,
Where he paused to listen and look down
A moment on the roofs of the town,
And the moonlight flowing over all.

Beneath in the churchyard, lay the dead,
In their night-encampment on the hill,
Wrapped in silence so deep and still
That he could hear, like a sentinel's tread,
The watchful night-wind, as it went
Creeping along from tent to tent,

And seeming to whisper, "All is Well!"
A moment only he feels the spell
Of the place and the hour, and the secret dread
Of the lonely belfry and the dead;
For suddenly all his thoughts are bent
On a shadowy something far away,
Where the river widens to meet the bay,—
A line of black that bends and floats
On the rising tide, like a bridge of boats.

Meanwhile, impatient to mount and ride,
Booted and spurred, with a heavy stride
On the opposite shore walked Paul Revere.
Now he patted his horse's side,
Now gazed at the landscape far and near,
Then, impetuous, stamped the earth,
And turned and tightened his saddle-girth;
But mostly he watched with eager search
The belfry-tower of the Old North Church,
As it rose above the graves on the hill,
Lonely and spectral and somber and still.
And lo! as he looks, on the belfry's height
A glimmer, and then a gleam of light!
He springs to the saddle, the bridle he turns,
But lingers and gazes, till full on his sight
A second lamp in the belfry burns!

A hurry of hoofs in a village street,
A shape in the moonlight, a bulk in the dark,
And beneath, from the pebbles, in passing, a spark
Struck out by a steed flying fearless and fleet:
That was all! And yet, through the gloom and the light,
The fate of a nation was riding that night;
And the spark struck out by that steed, in his flight
Kindled the land into flame with its heat.

He has left the village and mounted the steep,
And beneath him, tranquil and broad and deep,
Is the Mystic, meeting the ocean tides;
And under the alders that skirt its edge,
Now soft on the sand, now loud on the ledge,
Is heard the tramp of his steed as he rides.

It was twelve by the village clock,
When he crossed the bridge into Medford town.
He heard the crowing of the cock,
And the barking of the farmer's dog,
And felt the damp of the river fog,
That rises after the sun goes down.

It was one by the village clock,
When he galloped into Lexington.
He saw the gilded weathercock
Swim in the moonlight as he passed.
And the meeting-house windows, blank and bare,
Gaze at him with a spectral glare,
As if they already stood aghast
At the bloody work they would look upon.

It was two by the village clock,
When he came to the bridge in Concord town.
He heard the bleating of the flock,
And the twitter of birds among the trees,
And felt the breath of the morning breeze
Blowing over the meadows brown.
And one was safe and asleep in his bed
Who at the bridge would be first to fall,
Who that day would be lying dead,
Pierced by a British musket-ball.

You know the rest. In the books you have read,
How the British Regulars fired and fled,—

How the farmers gave them ball for ball,
From behind each fence and farmyard wall,
Chasing the red-coats down the lane,
Then crossing the fields to emerge again
Under the trees at the turn of the road,
And only pausing to fire and load.

So through the night rode Paul Revere;
And so through the night went his cry of alarm
To every Middlesex village and farm,—
A cry of defiance and not of fear,
A voice in the darkness, a knock at the door,
And a word that shall echo forevermore!
For, borne on the night-wind of the Past,
Through all our history, to the last,
In the hour of darkness and peril and need,
The people will waken and listen to hear
The hurrying hoof-beats of that steed,
And the midnight message of Paul Revere.

HENRY WADSWORTH LONGFELLOW

THE DEACON'S MASTERPIECE

Or, the Wonderful One-Hoss Shay

Have you heard of the wonderful one-hoss shay,
That was built in such a logical way
It ran a hundred years to a day,
And then of a sudden, it—ah, but stay,
I'll tell you what happened without delay,
Scaring the parson into fits,
Frightening people out of their wits,—
Have you ever heard of that, I say?

Seventeen hundred and fifty-five.
Georgius Secundus[1] was then alive,—
Snuffy old drone from the German hive.
That was the year when Lisbon-town
Saw the earth open and gulp her down,
And Braddock's army was done so brown,
Left without a scalp to its crown.
It was on the terrible Earthquake-day
That the Deacon finished the one-hoss shay.

Now in building of chaises,[2] I tell you what,
There is always *somewhere* a weakest spot,—
In hub, tire, felloe, in spring or thill,
In panel, or crossbar, floor, or sill,
In screw, bolt, thoroughbrace,—lurking still,
Find it somewhere you must and will;—
And that's the reason beyond a doubt,
That a chaise *breaks down,* but doesn't *wear out.*

But the Deacon swore (as Deacons do,
With an "I dew vum," or an "I tell yeou,")
He would build one shay to beat the taown
'n' the keounty 'n' all the kentry raoun';
It should be so built that it *couldn'* break daown:
—"Fur," said the Deacon, " 't's mighty plain
Thut the weakes' place mus' stan' the strain;
'n' the way t' fix it, uz I maintain,
          Is only jest
T'make that place uz strong uz the rest."

So the Deacon inquired of the village folk
Where he could find the strongest oak,
That couldn't be split nor bent nor broke,—
That was for spokes and floor and sills;
He sent for lancewood to make the thills;

[1] George the Second, King of England.   [2] Chaise: another name for shay.

The crossbars were ash, from the straightest trees,
The panels of white-wood, that cuts like cheese,
But lasts like iron for things like these;
The hubs of logs from the "Settler's ellum,"—
Last of its timber,—they couldn't sell 'em,
Never an ax had seen their chips,
And the wedges flew from between their lips,
Their blunt ends frizzled like celery-tips;
Step and prop-iron, bolt and screw,
Spring, tire, axle, and linchpin too,
Steel of the finest, bright and blue;
Thoroughbrace bison-skin, thick and wide;
Boot, top, dasher, from tough old hide
Found in the pit when the tanner died.
That was the way he "put her through."—
"There!" said the Deacon, *"naow* she'll dew!"

Do! I tell you, I rather guess
She was a wonder, and nothing less!
Colts grew horses, beards turned gray,
Deacon and deaconess dropped away,
Children and grandchildren—where were they?
But there stood the stout old one-hoss shay
As fresh as on Lisbon-earthquake-day!

Eighteen hundred;—it came and found
The Deacon's masterpiece strong and sound.
Eighteen hundred increased by ten;—
"Hahnsum kerridge" they called it then.
Eighteen hundred and twenty came;—
Running as usual; much the same.
Thirty and forty at last arrive,
And then come fifty, and fifty-five.

Little of all we value here
Wakes on the morn of its hundredth year
Without both feeling and looking queer.
In fact, there's nothing that keeps its youth,
So far as I know, but a tree and truth.
(This is a moral that runs at large;
Take it.—You're welcome.—No extra charge.)

First of November,—the Earthquake-day—
There are traces of age in the one-hoss shay,
A general flavor of mild decay,
But nothing local, as one may say.
There couldn't be,—for the Deacon's art
Had made it so like in every part
That there wasn't a chance for one to start.
For the wheels were just as strong as the thills,
And the floor was just as strong as the sills,
And the panels just as strong as the floor,
And the whipple-tree neither less nor more,
And the back-crossbar as strong as the fore,
And spring and axle and hub *encore.*[1]
And yet, *as a whole,* it is past a doubt
In another hour it will be *worn out!*

First of November, 'Fifty-five!
This morning the parson takes a drive.
Now, small boys, get out of the way!
Here comes the wonderful one-hoss shay,
Drawn by a rat-tailed, ewe-necked bay.
"Huddup!" said the parson.—Off went they.
The parson was working his Sunday's text,—
Had got to *fifthly,* and stopped perplexed
At what the—Moses!—was coming next.

---

[1] *Encore:* the same.

All at once the horse stood still,
Close by the meet'n'-house on the hill.
—First a shiver, and then a thrill,
Then something decidedly like a spill,—
And the parson was sitting upon a rock,
At half-past nine by the meet'n'-house clock.
Just the hour of the Earthquake shock!

—What do you think the parson found,
When he got up and stared around?
The poor old chaise in a heap or mound,
As if it had been to the mill and ground!
You see, of course, if you're not a dunce,
How it went to pieces all at once—
All at once, and nothing first—
Just as bubbles do when they burst.

End of the wonderful one-hoss shay.
Logic is logic. That's all I say.

OLIVER WENDELL HOLMES

CAP AND BELLS

CAP AND BELLS

After the guests had listened to the tall tales and heroic adventures in the great castles of the Middle Ages, someone came forward and began to make fun of the story-tellers. Or, instead of making fun of the tellers, he retold stories in such a way that the audience broke into laughter. Then he went further, making up legends of his own. Some of the legends sounded serious, some of them began truthfully; but there was always a wink in them, or a surprising twist, or a joking end before he finished. Usually he kept a straight and solemn face, but you could always tell he was the jester by the cap and bells he wore.

The poems in this group all wear cap and bells of one kind or another. In "The Owl-Critic" the bells have a light and teasing tinkle—"satire," I suppose, is the name for it. In "A Little Mistake" they ring out more laughably. In "The Diverting History of John Gilpin" (sometimes known as "John Gilpin's Ride") they break out into a loud and clattering peal.

One of the poems that amuses me most is "The Naughty Boy." I enjoy it not because it is the funniest, but because it was written by a great poet, John Keats, who was anything but a jester and who was far too serious to wear the merry cap and jingling bells except once or twice in his life.

"A Tragic Story"—which is really not the least bit tragic—comes to us in a most roundabout way. It was composed by a French poet who wrote in German, and it was made over by an Englishman who is better known for his novels than for his poetry. No one who reads "Vanity Fair" and "The Newcomes" needs to be told anything about Thackeray.

"A Legend of Lake Okeefinokee" is one of those merry tunes of my youth. There's no doubt about the bells here—even the word "Okeefinokee" has a tinkle of its own. Don't let the title of "A Sad, Sad Story" fool you; it is, as you will quickly see, nothing more than a joke, and I don't think the man who wrote it—some say it was Oliver Goldsmith, who wrote "An Elegy on the

Death of a Mad Dog" on page 239—meant you to weep about the children who fell through the ice. I don't even believe they were drowned. They were probably badly frightened and developed nasty colds and had to stay in bed for a week, which Taught them a Lesson.

So with "How the Babes in the Wood Showed They Couldn't Be Beaten." Here, too, is a laughing legend with a lesson at the end. You have, probably, read the serious poem on page 265. Here is the jester's way of treating that tale.

THE OWL-CRITIC

"Who stuffed that white owl?" No one spoke in the shop:
The barber was busy and he couldn't stop;
The customers waiting their turns, were all reading
The *Daily,* the *Herald,* the *Post,* little heeding
The young man who blurted out such a blunt question;
Not one raised a head, or even made a suggestion;
    And the barber kept on shaving.

"Don't you see, Mister Brown,"
Cried the youth with a frown,
"How wrong the whole thing is,
How preposterous each wing is,
How flattened the head is, how jammed down the neck is—
In short, the whole owl, what an ignorant wreck 'tis!
I make no apology;
I've learned owl-eology.
I've passed days and nights in a hundred collections,
And cannot be blinded to any defections
Arising from unskillful fingers that fail
To stuff a bird right, from his beak to his tail.
Mister Brown! Mister Brown!
Do take that bird down,
Or you'll soon be the laughing-stock all over town!"
    And the barber kept on shaving.

"I've *studied* owls
And other night fowls,
And I tell you
What I know to be true:
An owl cannot roost
With his limbs so unloosed;

Rainbow in the Sky

No owl in this world
Ever had his claws curled,
Ever had his legs slanted,
Ever had his bill canted,
Ever had his neck screwed
Into that attitude.
He can't *do* it, because
'Tis against all bird-laws.
Anatomy teaches,
Ornithology preaches
An owl has a toe
That *can't* turn out so!
I've made the white owl my study for years,
And to see such a job almost moves me to tears!
Mister Brown, I'm amazed
You should be so crazed
As to put up a bird
In that posture absurd!
To *look* at that owl really brings on a dizziness;
The man who stuffed *him* don't half know his business!"
    And the barber kept on shaving.

"Examine those eyes.
I'm filled with surprise
Taxidermists should pass
Off on you such poor glass;
So unnatural they seem
They'd make Audubon [1] scream,
And John Burroughs [1] laugh
To encounter such chaff.
Do take that bird down;
Have him stuffed again, Mr. Brown!"
    And the barber kept on shaving.

[1] Audubon and Burroughs were two famous nature-lovers and students of animal life.

"With some sawdust and bark
I could stuff in the dark
An owl better than that.
I could make an old hat
Look more like an owl
Than that horrid fowl,
Stuck up there so stiff like a side of coarse leather.
In fact, about *him* there's not one natural feather."
    And the barber kept on shaving.

Just then with a wink and a sly normal lurch,
The owl very gravely got down from his perch,
Walked round, and regarded his fault-finding critic
(Who thought he was stuffed) with a glance analytic
And then fairly hooted, as if he would say:
"Your learning's at fault *this* time, anyway;
Don't waste it again on a live bird I pray.
I'm an owl; you're another. Sir Critic, good-day!"
    And the barber kept on shaving.

JAMES THOMAS FIELDS

THE NAUGHTY BOY

There was a naughty boy,
  And a naughty boy was he,
He ran away to Scotland
  The people for to see—
    Then he found
    That the ground
    Was as hard,
    That a yard
    Was as long,
    That a song
    Was as merry,
    That a cherry
    Was as red—

That lead
Was as weighty,
That fourscore
Was as eighty,
That a door
Was as wooden
  As in England—
So he stood in his shoes
  And he wondered,
  He wondered.
He stood in his shoes
  And he wondered.

JOHN KEATS

THE DIVERTING HISTORY OF JOHN GILPIN

*Showing How He Went Farther Than He Intended, and Came
Safe Home Again*

I

John Gilpin was a citizen
    Of credit and renown,
A train-band Captain eke[1] was he
    Of famous London town.

John Gilpin's spouse said to her dear,
    "Though wedded we have been
These twice ten tedious years, yet we
    No holiday have seen.

Tomorrow is our wedding day,
    And we will then repair
Unto the Bell at Edmonton,
    All in a chaise and pair.

My sister and my sister's child,
    Myself and children three,
Will fill the chaise; so you must ride
    On horseback after we."

He soon replied,—"I do admire
    Of womankind, but one,
And you are she, my dearest dear,
    Therefore it shall be done.

[1] "Eke" is an old word meaning "also."

326

I am a linen-draper bold,
  As all the world doth know,
And my good friend the Calender
  Will lend his horse to go."

Quoth Mrs. Gilpin,—"That's well said,
  And for that wine is dear,
We will be furnish'd with our own,
  Which is both bright and clear."

John Gilpin kiss'd his loving wife;
  O'erjoyed was he to find
That though on pleasure she was bent,
  She had a frugal mind.

The morning came, the chaise was brought,
  But yet was not allow'd
To drive up to the door, lest all
  Should say that she was proud.

So three doors off the chaise was stay'd,
  Where they did all get in;
Six precious souls, and all agog
  To dash through thick and thin.

Smack went the whip, round went the wheels,
  Were never folk so glad,
The stones did rattle underneath
  As if Cheapside were mad.

John Gilpin at his horse's side,
  Seized fast the flowing mane,
And up he got, in haste to ride,
  But soon came down again;

NOW SEE HIM MOUNTED ONCE AGAIN

For saddle-tree scarce reach'd had he,
   His journey to begin,
When, turning round his head, he saw
   Three customers come in.

So down he came; for loss of time,
   Although it grieved him sore,
Yet loss of pence, full well he knew,
   Would trouble him much more.

'T was long before the customers
   Were suited to their mind,
When Betty, screaming, came downstairs,
   "The wine is left behind!"

"Good lack!" quoth he, "yet bring it me,
   My leathern belt likewise,
In which I bear my trusty sword
   When I do exercise."

Now Mistress Gilpin, careful soul!
   Had two stone bottles found,
To hold the liquor that she loved,
   And keep it safe and sound.

Each bottle had a curling ear,
   Through which the belt he drew,
And hung a bottle on each side,
   To make his balance true.

Then over all, that he might be
   Equipp'd from top to toe,
His long red cloak, well brush'd and neat,
   He manfully did throw.

Now see him mounted once again
   Upon his nimble steed,
Full slowly pacing o'er the stones
   With caution and good heed.

329

But, finding soon a smoother road
   Beneath his well-shod feet,
The snorting beast began to trot,
   Which gall'd him in his seat,

So "Fair and softly," John he cried,
   But John he cried in vain;
That trot became a gallop soon,
   In spite of curb and rein.

So stooping down, as needs he must
   Who cannot sit upright,
He grasp'd the mane with both his hands,
   And eke with all his might.

His horse, who never in that sort
　　Had handled been before,
What thing upon his back had got
　　Did wonder more and more.

Away went Gilpin, neck or nought,
　　Away went hat and wig!
He little dreamt when he set out
　　Of running such a rig!

The wind did blow, the cloak did fly,
　　Like streamer long and gay,
Till, loop and button failing both,
　　At last it flew away.

Then might all people well discern
   The bottles he had slung;
A bottle swinging at each side,
   As hath been said or sung.

The dogs did bark, the children scream'd,
   Up flew the windows all,
And ev'ry soul cried out, "Well done!"
   As loud as he could bawl.

Away went Gilpin—who but he?
   His fame soon spread around—
"He carries weight!" "He rides a race!"
   " 'T is for a thousand pound!"

And still, as fast as he drew near,
   'T was wonderful to view,
How in a trice the turnpike-men
   Their gates wide open threw.

And now, as he went bowing down
   His reeking head full low,
The bottles twain behind his back
   Were shattered at a blow.

Down ran the wine into the road,
   Most piteous to be seen,
Which made his horse's flanks to smoke
   As they had basted been.

But still he seem'd to carry weight,
   With leathern girdle braced,
For all might see the bottle-necks
   Still dangling at his waist.

Thus all through merry Islington
  These gambols he did play,
Until he came unto the Wash
  Of Edmonton so gay.

And there he threw the Wash about
  On both sides of the way,
Just like unto a trundling mop,
  Or a wild-goose at play.

At Edmonton his loving wife
  From the balcony spied
Her tender husband, wond'ring much
  To see how he did ride.

"Stop, stop, John Gilpin!—Here's the house!"
  They all at once did cry;
"The dinner waits and we are tired:"
  Said Gilpin—"So am I!"

But yet his horse was not a whit
  Inclined to tarry there;
For why? His owner had a house
  Full ten miles off, at Ware,

So like an arrow swift he flew,
  Shot by an archer strong;
So did he fly—which brings me to
  The middle of my song.

II

Away went Gilpin, out of breath,
  And sore against his will,
Till at his friend the Calender's
  His horse at last stood still.

The Calender, amazed to see
    His neighbor in such trim,
Laid down his pipe, flew to the gate,
    And thus accosted him:—

"What news? what news? your tidings tell,
    Tell me you must and shall—
Say why bare-headed you are come,
    Or why you come at all?"

Now Gilpin had a pleasant wit,
    And loved a timely joke,
And thus unto the Calender
    In merry guise he spoke:—

"I came because your horse would come;
    And if I well forebode,
My hat and wig will soon be here,
    They are upon the road."

The Calender, right glad to find
    His friend in merry pin,
Return'd him not a single word,
    But to the house went in;

Whence straight he came with hat and wig,
    A wig that flow'd behind,
A hat not much the worse for wear,
    Each comely in its kind.

He held them up, and in his turn
    Thus show'd his ready wit:—
"My head is twice as big as yours,
    They therefore needs must fit.

STRAIGHT HE CAME WITH HAT AND WIG

But let me scrape the dirt away
    That hangs upon your face;
And stop and eat, for well you may
    Be in a hungry case."

Said John, "It is my wedding-day,
    And all the world would stare,
If wife should dine at Edmonton,
    And I should dine at Ware."

So, turning to his horse, he said—
    "I am in haste to dine;
'T was for your pleasure you came here,
    You shall go back for mine."

Ah, luckless speech and bootless boast!
    For which he paid full dear;
For, while he spake, a braying ass
    Did sing most loud and clear;

Whereat his horse did snort, as he
    Had heard a lion roar,
And gallop'd off with all his might,
    As he had done before.

Away went Gilpin, and away
    Went Gilpin's hat and wig!
He lost them sooner than at first,
    For why?—they were too big!

Now Mistress Gilpin, when she saw
    Her husband posting down
Into the country far away,
    She pull'd out half-a-crown;

FOR, WHILE HE SPAKE, A BRAYING ASS DID SING MOST
LOUD AND CLEAR

And thus unto the youth she said
    That drove them to the Bell—
"This shall be yours when you bring back
    My husband safe and well."

The youth did ride, and soon did meet
    John coming back amain;
Whom in a trice he tried to stop,
    By catching at his rein;

But not performing what he meant,
    And gladly would have done,
The frighted steed he frighted more,
    And made him faster run.

Away went Gilpin, and away
   Went post-boy at his heels!—
The post-boy's horse right glad to miss
   The lumb'ring of the wheels.

Six gentlemen upon the road,
   Thus seeing Gilpin fly,
With post-boy scamp'ring in the rear,
   They raised the hue and cry:—

"Stop thief! stop thief! A highwayman!"
   Not one of them was mute.
And all and each that pass'd that way
   Did join in the pursuit.

And now the turnpike gates again
   Flew open in short space;
The toll-men thinking, as before,
   That Gilpin rode a race.

And so he did, and won it too,
   For he got first to town;
Nor stopp'd till where he had got up
   He did again get down.

Now let us sing, Long live the king,
   And Gilpin, long live he;
And when he next doth ride abroad,
   May I be there to see!

WILLIAM COWPER

A LEGEND OF LAKE OKEEFINOKEE

There once was a frog,
And he lived in a bog,
On the banks of Lake Okeefinokee.
And the words of the song
That he sang all day long
Were, "Croakety croakety croaky."

Said the frog, "I have found
That my life's daily round
In this place is exceedingly poky.
So no longer I'll stop,
But I swiftly will hop
Away from Lake Okeefinokee."

Now a bad mocking-bird
By mischance overheard
The words of the frog as he spokee.
And he said, "All my life
Frog and I've been at strife,
As we lived by Lake Okeefinokee.

"Now I see at a glance
Here's a capital chance
For to play him a practical jokee.
So I'll venture to say
That he shall not today
Leave the banks of Lake Okeefinokee."

So this bad mocking-bird,
Without saying a word,
He flew to a tree which was oaky;
And loudly he sang,
Till the whole forest rang,
"Oh! Croakety croakety croaky!"

As he warbled this song,
Master Frog came along,
A-filling his pipe for to smokee;
And he said, " 'Tis some frog
Has escaped from the bog
Of Okeefinokee-finokee.

"I am filled with amaze
To hear one of my race
A-warbling on top of an oaky;
But if frogs can climb trees,
I may still find some ease
On the banks of Lake Okeefinokee."

So he climbed up the tree;
But alas! down fell he!
And his lovely green neck it was brokee;
And the sad truth to say,
Never more did he stray
From the banks of Lake Okeefinokee.

And the bad mocking-bird
Said, "How very absurd
And delightful a practical jokee!"
But I'm happy to say
He was drowned the next day
In the waters of Okeefinokee.

LAURA E. RICHARDS

341

A LITTLE MISTAKE

I studied my tables over and over, and backward and forward, too;
But I couldn't remember six times nine, and I didn't know what to do,
Till sister told me to play with my doll, and not to bother my head.
"If you call her 'Fifty-four' for a while, you'll learn it by heart," she said.

So I took my favorite Mary Ann (though I thought 'twas a dreadful shame
To give such a perfectly lovely child such a perfectly horrid name),
And I called her my dear little "Fifty-four" a hundred times, till I knew
The answer of six times nine as well as the answer of six times two.

Next day, Elizabeth Wigglesworth, who always seems so proud,
Said, "Six times nine is fifty-two," and I nearly laughed aloud!
But I wished I hadn't when teacher said, "Now, Dorothy, tell if you can,"
For I thought of my doll, and—oh dear me!—I answered "Mary Ann!"

ANNA M. PRATT

THE BALLAD OF THE MERRY FERRY

Sing hey, and sing ho, and sing down-a-down-derry,
Oh, what is so merry
As missing the ferry!

A nice wintry morning
So jolly and freezing.
A dear little cold keeps you coughing and sneezing;
And everyone mirthful and happy and gay,
As we all watch the ferry go puffing away.

Sing hey, and sing ho, and sing down-a-down-derry,
Oh, what is so merry
As missing the ferry!

EMMA ROUNDS

A TRAGIC STORY

There lived a sage in days of yore,
And he a handsome pigtail wore;
But wondered much and sorrowed more,
   Because it hung behind him.

He mused upon the curious case,
And swore he'd change the pigtail's place,
And have it hanging at his face,
   Not dangling there behind him.

Says he, "The mystery I've found—
I'll turn me round"—he turned him round;
   But still it hung behind him.

Then round and round and out and in,
All day the puzzled sage did spin;
In vain—it mattered not a pin—
   The pigtail hung behind him.

And right and left, and round about,
And up and down and in and out
He turned; but still the pigtail stout
   Hung steadily behind him.

And though his efforts never slack,
And though he twist, and twirl, and tack,
Alas! still faithful to his back,
   The pigtail stands behind him.

WILLIAM MAKEPEACE THACKERAY
*Adapted from the German
of Adelbert von Chamisso*

A SAD, SAD STORY

Three children sliding on the ice
    Upon a summer's day,
As it fell out they all fell in,
    The rest they ran away.

Oh! had these children been at school,
    Or sliding on dry ground,
Ten thousand pounds to one penny
    They had not then been drowned.

You parents who have children dear,
    And you that have got none,
If you would keep them safe abroad,
    Pray keep them safe at home.

WHEN I WAS A BACHELOR

When I was a bachelor
    I lived by myself,
And all the bread and cheese I got
    I laid upon the shelf;
The rats and the mice
    They made such a strife,
That I was forced to go to town
    And buy me a wife.

The streets were so broad,
    The lanes were so narrow,
I had to bring her home
    In an old wheel-barrow;
The wheel-barrow broke,
    And my wife had a fall.
Down tumbled
    Wheel-barrow, wife, and all.

HOW THE BABES IN THE WOOD SHOWED THEY COULDN'T BE BEATEN [1]

A man of kind and noble mind
    Was H. Gustavus Hyde.

[1] The original, and serious, version of this tale is on page 265.

'Twould be amiss to add to this
   At present, for he died,
In full possession of his senses,
The day before my tale commences.

One half his gold his four-year-old-
   Son Paul was known to win,
And Beatrix, whose age was six,
   For all the rest came in,
Perceiving which, their Uncle Ben did
A thing that people said was splendid.

For by the hand he took them, and
   Remarked in accents smooth:
"One thing I ask. Be mine the task
   These stricken babes to soothe!
My country home is really charming:
I'll teach them all the joys of farming."

Concealing guile beneath a smile,
   He took them to a wood,
And, with severe and most austere
   Injunctions to be good,
He left them seated on a gateway,
And took his own departure straightway.

Though much afraid, the children stayed
   From ten till nearly eight;
At times they wept, at times they slept,
   But never left the gate:
Until the swift suspicion crossed them
That Uncle Benjamin had lost them.

Then, quite unnerved, young Paul observed:
    "It's like a dreadful dream,
And Uncle Ben has fallen ten
    Per cent in my esteem.
Not only did he first usurp us,
But now he's left us here on purpose!"

*   *   *   *

For countless years their childish fears
    Have made the reader pale,
For countless years the public's tears
    Have started at the tale,
For countless years much detestation
Has been expressed for their relation.

So draw a veil across the dale
    Where stood that ghastly gate.
No need to tell. You know full well
    What was their touching fate,
And how with leaves each little dead breast
Was covered by a Robin Redbreast!

But when they found them on the ground,
    Although their life had ceased
Quite near to Paul there lay a small
    White paper, neatly creased.
*"Because of lack of any merit,
B. Hyde,"* it ran, *"we disinherit!"*

The Moral: If you deeply long
To punish one who's done you wrong,
Though in your lifetime fail you may,
Where there's a Will, there is a way!

GUY WETMORE CARRYL

SIMPLY NONSENSE

SIMPLY NONSENSE

"Life is real, life is earnest," wrote an American poet, and we all agree with him. But an older poet has said:

> A little nonsense now and then
> Is relished by the best of men.

That is more comforting, for we can't be earnest and serious all the time. There are times when the mind as well as the body feels like kicking up its heels and enjoying itself without care—even without thought.

The verses in this section are for such times. You are not to think too much about them—in fact you are not to think at all. If you try to find the meaning of the lines, you will lose all the pleasure, for they have no meaning. Instead of meaning, they have music—the music of strange and lovely sounds, of queer rhymes and queerer rhythms. There is a pleasure, and I think a great one, in the beauty of sound quite apart from sense. After all, we enjoy a concert or the beat of a band without asking what the music *means*.

Of course not everyone cares for nonsense; a few want nothing but facts and figures. But even those of us who are such "realists" must chuckle at some of the nonsensical old rhymes and the new ones by Laura E. Richards, Gelett Burgess, and Michael Lewis; only a rare few cannot enjoy the ridiculous ideas in the limericks.

Speaking of limericks, the inventor of them, Edward Lear, was one of the greatest, possibly *the* greatest writer of nonsense verse. I would have liked to print all of his nonsense books, including his nonsense alphabet, but there was scarcely room for all the poems I have chosen. But I did manage to crowd in a few of my favorites—especially "The Owl and the Pussy-cat," "The Quangle Wangle's Hat," "The Jumblies," "The Akond of Swat," and "Mr. Lear," in which the poet makes fun of himself.

All the nonsense poems should be spoken, not merely read; but "The

349

Akond of Swat" is a piece that just *has* to be read out loud. It doesn't mean anything, although I've been told that there *is* such a place as Swat somewhere in India and that the ruler *is* called the Akond. At any rate, the sound of the poem matters even if the meaning doesn't, and the proper way to read the verses is to shout the words at the end of each line—the little words printed in capitals. If the words can be shouted out by two or three people, or a whole chorus, so much the better.

Then there is the wonderful nonsense poetry in "Alice in Wonderland" and "Through the Looking Glass." You will find one of the poems, "The Lobster's Quadrille," on page 258; two more of the "Alice" poems, and a third by their author, are in this section. At the very end I have put a nonsense "tester"—the most meaningless piece of prose-poetry ever written. "The Great Panjandrum Himself" is the wildest lot of words collected in eighteen lines and people either learn it by heart—relishing every word and declaiming "What! no soap?"—or they regard it as just silly. It is, as I said, a test whether you like nonsense or not.

But before you sneer at nonsense, let me tell you an interesting fact. The best and most beloved nonsense verse was written by Edward Lear and Lewis Carroll—and both men were respected for their serious work. Edward Lear traveled, painted, and illustrated heavy books; Lewis Carroll, under his real name, Charles L. Dodgson, was a teacher of mathematics. Yet the nonsense verses of Edward Lear are more celebrated today than his "Journals of a Landscape Painter" or his hundreds of drawings; Carroll's "Alice" is in every home, while his solemn works on geometry are happily forgotten.

And that, I think, is just as it should be.

OLD NURSERY NONSENSE

There was an old man,
   And he had a calf,
   And that's half.

He took him from the stall,
   And put him on the wall,
   And that's all.

Three wise men of Gotham,
They went to sea in a bowl.
If the bowl had been stronger,
My song would be longer.

There was an old woman
   Lived under a hill,
And if she hasn't left there,
   She lives there still.

There was an old woman
   Lived up on a hill,
She put a mouse in a bag
   And sent it to mill.

The miller did swear
   By the point of his knife,
He never had ground up
   A mouse in his life.

Ding, dong, bell,
Pussy's in the well.
Who put her in?
Little Johnny Green.
What a naughty boy was that,
To drown a little pussy cat,
Who never did him any harm,
But killed the mice in his father's barn.

There was a crooked man and he went a crooked mile,
He found a crooked sixpence against a crooked stile,
He bought a crooked cat, which caught a crooked mouse,
And they all lived together in a crooked little house.

See-saw, Margery Daw,
    Jacky shall have a new master;
Jacky shall have but a penny a day,
    Because he can't work any faster.

Great A, little a,
    Bouncing B;
The cat's in the cupboard
    And can't see me.

Little Tommy Tucker
Sings for his supper.
What shall he eat?
White bread and butter.
How will he cut it
Without any knife?
And how will he be married
Without any wife?

Pease-porridge hot,
Pease-porridge cold,
Pease-porridge in the pot
Nine days old.

Some like it hot,
Some like it cold,
Some like it in the pot
Nine days old.

Pat a cake, pat a cake,
Baker's man,
Bake me a cake
As fast as you can.
Pat it, and prick it,
And mark it with D,
And put it in the oven
For Dicky and me.

Jack Sprat
    Could eat no fat,
His wife could eat no lean;
    And so between
    The two of them
They licked the platter clean.

ODD FELLOWS

"Old woman, old woman, shall we go a-shearing?"
"Speak a little louder, sir, I am very hard of hearing."
"Old woman, old woman, shall I love you dearly?"
"Thank you, kind sir, I hear you very clearly."

Old Abram Brown is dead and gone,
   You'll never see him more;
He used to wear a long brown coat,
   That buttoned down before.

There was an old woman tossed up in a basket
   Nineteen times as high as the moon;
Where she was going I couldn't but ask it,
   For in her hand she carried a broom.

"Old woman, old woman, old woman," quoth I,
   "O whither, O whither, O whither, so high?"
"To brush the cobwebs off the sky!"
   "Shall I go with thee?" "Ay, by-and-by."

'TIS MIDNIGHT

'Tis midnight, and the setting sun
   Is slowly rising in the west;
The rapid rivers slowly run,
   The frog is on his downy nest.
The pensive goat and sportive cow,
Hilarious leap from bough to bough.

FOOD FOR THOUGHT

Cataline, Cato,
Pericles and Plato,
All they could eat
Was cold boiled potato.

Mumbo, Jumbo,
Christopho Columbo,
Came to America
For New Orleans gumbo.

Rikki-tikki-tavy,
Solomon and Davie,
Lived for months
On roast beef and gravy.

Niminy, piminy,
Francesca de Rimini,
Whatever she ate
She ate in the chiminee!

MICHAEL LEWIS

NONSENSE SONG

Oh, tell me what you see,
Oh, tell me what you see;
What is that lumbering thing you see,
Hum, dum, thing you see,
Oh, tell me what you see.

It is a bumble-bee,
It is a bumble-bee,
It is a lumbering bumble-bee,
Hum, dum, bumble-bee,
It is a bumble-bee.

What may his number be?
What may his number be?
What may his lumbering number be?
Hum, dum, number be?
What may his number be?

Eleven hundred and three.
Eleven hundred and three.
Eleven hundred and lumbering three;
Hum, dum, hundred and three.
Eleven hundred and three.

GERMAN STUDENT-SONG
Adapted by Michael Lewis

NONSENSE VERSES

I

Nicholas Ned,
He lost his head,
And put a turnip on instead;
But then, ah, me!
He could not see,
So he thought it was night, and he went to bed.

II

Ponsonby Perks,
  He fought the Turks,
Performing many wonderful works;
  He killed over forty,
  High-minded and haughty,
And cut off their heads with smiles and smirks.

III

Winifred White,
  She married a fright,
She called him her darling, her duck, and delight;
  The back of his head
  Was so lovely, she said,
It dazzled her soul and enraptured her sight.

IV

Harriet Hutch,
  Her conduct was such,
Her uncle remarked it would conquer the Dutch;
  She boiled her new bonnet,
  And breakfasted on it,
And rode to the moon on her grandmother's crutch.

LAURA E. RICHARDS

QUEER QUATRAINS

The Roof it has a Lazy Time
  A-Lying in the Sun;
The Walls, they have to Hold Him Up;
  They do Not Have Much Fun!

I'd Never Dare to Walk Across
  A Bridge I Could Not See,
For Quite Afraid of Falling off
  I Fear that I Should Be!

My Feet they haul me Round the House,
  They Hoist me up the Stairs;
I only have to Steer them, and
  They Ride me Everywheres!

My House is Made of Graham Bread,
  Except the Ceiling's Made of White;
Of Angel Cake I make my Bed—
  I eat my Pillow Every Night!

GELETT BURGESS

BOBBY BINGO

The miller's dog lay at the door,
  And his name was Bobby Bingo:
B with an I, I with an N, N with a G, G with an O,
  His name was Bobby Bingo.

357

Rainbow in the Sky

The miller he bought a barrel of ale,
And he called it right good Stingo:
S with a T, T with an I, I with an N, N with a G, G with an O,
He called it right good Stingo.

The miller he went to town one day,
And he bought a wedding ring-o:
R with an I, I with an N, N with a G, G with an O,
He bought a wedding ring-o.

The miller, he took it home to his dog,
And his dog was Bobby Bingo:
B with an I, I with an N, N with a G, G with an O,
His name was Bobby Bingo.

OH! SUSANNA!

I come from Alabama, with my banjo on my knee;
I'm going to Louisiana, my true love for to see.
It rained all night the day I left, the weather was so dry;
The sun so hot I froze to death. Susanna, don't you cry.
Oh! Susanna! Don't you cry for me;
I've come from Alabama with my banjo on my knee.

I had a dream the other night when everything was still;
I thought I saw Susanna a-coming down the hill.
A buckwheat cake was in her mouth, a tear was in her eye.
Says I, "I'm coming from the South, Susanna, don't you cry."
Oh! Susanna! Don't you cry for me;
I've come from Alabama with my banjo on my knee.

AMERICAN MINSTREL SONG

SOME OLD LIMERICKS

A man went a-hunting at Rygate,
And wished to leap over a high gate.
 Said the owner, "Go 'round,
 With your gun and your hound,
For you never shall leap over *my* gate!"

There was a fat man of Bombay,
Who was smoking one sunshiny day,
 When a bird, called a snipe,
 Flew away with his pipe
Which vexed the fat man of Bombay.

There was an old woman of Leeds,
Who spent all her time in good deeds.
 She worked for the poor
 Till her fingers were sore,
This pious old woman of Leeds.

There was an old man of Tobago,
Who lived just on gruel and sago,
 Till, much to his bliss,
 His physician said this:
"To a fat leg of mutton you *may* go."

LEAR'S LIMERICKS

There was an Old Man of the West,
Who never could get any rest;
    So they set him to spin
    On his nose and his chin,
Which cured that Old Man of the West.

There was an Old Man of the Coast
Who placidly sat on a post;
    But when it grew cold
    He relinquished his hold,
And called for some hot buttered toast.

There was a Young Lady whose chin
Resembled the point of a pin:
    So she had it made sharp,
    And purchased a harp,
And played several tunes with her chin.

There was an Old Man, who said, "Well!
Will *nobody* answer this bell?
    I have pulled day and night,
    Till my hair has grown white,
But nobody answers this bell!"

There was a Young Lady whose eyes
Were unique as to color and size;
   When she opened them wide,
   People all turned aside,
And started away in surprise.

There was an Old Person of Burton,
Whose answers were rather uncertain;
   When they said, "How d'ye do?"
   He replied, "Who are you?"
That distressing Old Person of Burton.

There was an Old Lady whose folly
Induced her to sit in a holly;
   Whereon by a thorn,
   Her dress being torn,
She quickly became melancholy.

There was an Old Man who supposed
That the street door was partially closed;
   But some very large rats
   Ate his coats and his hats,
While that futile old gentleman dozed.

EDWARD LEAR

NEW NONSENSE LIMERICKS

There once was a boy of Bagdad,
An inquisitive sort of a lad.
　　He said, "I will see
　　If a sting has a bee."
And he very soon found that it had.

There was an old lady of Wales,
Who lived upon oysters and snails.
　　Upon growing a shell,
　　She exclaimed, "It is well,
I won't have to wear bonnets or veils."

A funny old person of Slough
Took all of his meals with a cow.
　　He said, "It's uncanny,
　　She's *so* like Aunt Fanny!"
But he never would indicate how.

There was a young farmer of Leeds,
Who swallowed six packets of seeds.
　　It soon came to pass
　　He was covered with grass,
And he couldn't sit down for the weeds.

There was a young fellow of Perth,
Who was born on the day of his birth;
   He was married, they say
   On his wife's wedding day,
And he died when he quitted the earth.

A diner while dining at Crewe
Found quite a large mouse in his stew.
   Said the waiter, "Don't shout,
   And wave it about,
Or the rest will be wanting one, too!"

There was an old lady who said,
When she found a thief under her bed,
   "Get up from the floor;
   You're too close to the door,
And I fear you'll take cold in the head."

There was an old man who said, "Do
Tell me *how* I should add two and two?
   I think more and more
   That it makes about four—
But I fear that is almost too few."

There was a young maid who said, "Why
Can't I look in my ear with my eye?
    If I give my mind to it,
    I'm sure I can do it.
You never can tell till you try."

MR. LEAR

"How pleasant to know Mr. Lear!"
    Who has written such volumes of stuff!
Some think him ill-tempered and queer,
    But a few think him pleasant enough.

His mind is concrete and fastidious,
    His nose is remarkably big;
His visage is more or less hideous,
    His beard it resembles a wig.

He has ears, and two eyes, and ten fingers,
    Leastways if you reckon two thumbs;
Long ago he was one of the singers,
    But now he is one of the dumbs.

He sits in a beautiful parlor,
    With hundreds of books on the wall;
He drinks a great deal of Marsala,
    But never gets tipsy at all.

He has many friends, lay men and clerical,
  Old Foss is the name of his cat;
His body is perfectly spherical,
  He weareth a runcible hat.

When he walks out in waterproof white,
  The children run after him so!
Calling out, "He's come out in his night-
  Gown, that old Englishman, oh!"

He weeps by the side of the ocean,
  He weeps on the top of the hill;
He purchases pancake and lotion,
  And chocolate shrimps from the mill.

He reads, but he cannot speak, Spanish,
  He cannot abide ginger-beer:
Ere the days of his pilgrimage vanish,
  How pleasant to know Mr. Lear!

                                   EDWARD LEAR

THE OWL AND THE PUSSY-CAT

The Owl and the Pussy-Cat went to sea
   In a beautiful pea-green boat:
They took some honey, and plenty of money
   Wrapped up in a five-pound note.
The Owl looked up to the stars above,
   And sang to a small guitar,
"O lovely Pussy, O Pussy, my love,
   What a beautiful Pussy you are,
         You are,
         You are!
What a beautiful Pussy you are!"

Pussy said to the Owl, "You elegant fowl,
　　How charmingly sweet you sing!
Oh! let us be married; too long we have tarried!
　　But what shall we do for a ring?"
They sailed away, for a year and a day,
　　To the land where the bong-tree grows;
And there in a wood a Piggy-wig stood,
　　With a ring at the end of his nose,
　　　　　　His nose,
　　　　　　His nose,
　　With a ring at the end of his nose.

"Dear Pig, are you willing to sell for one shilling
 Your ring?" Said the Piggy, "I will."
So they took it away, and were married next day
 By the turkey who lives on the hill.
They dined on mince and slices of quince,
 Which they ate with a runcible spoon;
And hand in hand, on the edge of the sand,
 They danced by the light of the moon
   The moon,
   The moon,
 They danced by the light of the moon.

EDWARD LEAR

THE JUMBLIES

They went to sea in a sieve, they did;
   In a sieve they went to sea:
In spite of all their friends could say,
On a winter's morn, on a stormy day,
   In a sieve they went to sea.
And when the sieve turned round and round,
And everyone cried, "You'll all be drowned!"
They called aloud, "Our sieve ain't big;
But we don't care a button, we don't care a fig:
   In a sieve we'll go to sea!"
     Far and few, far and few,
       Are the lands where the Jumblies live:
      Their heads are green, and their hands are blue;
       And they went to sea in a sieve.

They sailed away in a sieve, they did,
   In a sieve they sailed so fast,
With only a beautiful pea-green veil
Tied with a ribbon, by way of a sail,
   To a small tobacco-pipe mast.
And everyone said who saw them go,
"Oh! won't they be soon upset, you know?
For the sky is dark, and the voyage is long;
And, happen what may, it's extremely wrong
   In a sieve to sail so fast."
     Far and few, far and few,
       Are the lands where the Jumblies live;
      Their heads are green, and their hands are blue;
       And they went to sea in a sieve.

The water it soon came in, it did;
    The water it soon came in:
So, to keep them dry, they wrapped their feet
In a pinky paper all folded neat;
    And they fastened it down with a pin.
And they passed the night in a crockery-jar;
And each of them said, "How wise we are!
Though the sky be dark, and the voyage be long,
Yet we never can think we were rash or wrong,
    While round in our sieve we spin."
        Far and few, far and few,
           Are the lands where the Jumblies live:
           Their heads are green, and their hands are blue;
           And they went to sea in a sieve.

And all night long they sailed away;
    And when the sun went down,
They whistled and warbled a moony song
To the echoing sound of a coppery gong,
    In the shade of the mountains brown.
"O Timballoo! How happy we are
When we live in a sieve and a crockery-jar!
And all night long, in the moonlight pale,
We sail away with a pea-green sail
    In the shade of the mountains brown."
        Far and few, far and few,
           Are the lands where the Jumblies live:
           Their heads are green, and their hands are blue;
           And they went to sea in a sieve.

They sailed to the Western Sea, they did,—
    To a land all covered with trees:
And they bought an owl and a useful cart,
And a pound of rice, and a cranberry-tart,
    And a hive of silvery bees;
And they bought a pig, and some green jackdaws,
And a lovely monkey with lollipop paws,
And forty bottles of ring-bo-ree,
    And no end of Stilton cheese.
        Far and few, far and few,
            Are the lands where the Jumblies live:
        Their heads are green, and their hands are blue;
            And they went to sea in a sieve.

And in twenty years they all came back,—
    In twenty years or more;
And everyone said, "How tall they've grown!
For they've been to the Lakes, and the Torrible Zone,
    And the hills of the Chankly Bore."
And they drank their health, and gave them a feast
Of dumplings made of beautiful yeast;
And everyone said, "If we only live,
We, too, will go to sea in a sieve,
    To the hills of the Chankly Bore."
        Far and few, far and few,
            Are the lands where the Jumblies live:
        Their heads are green, and their hands are blue;
            And they went to sea in a sieve.

                                        EDWARD LEAR

371

THE AKOND OF SWAT

Who, or why, or which, or what   Is the Akond of Swat?

Is he tall or short, or dark, or fair?
Does he sit on a stool or a sofa or chair,   or SQUAT,
                                                 The Akond of Swat?

Is he wise or foolish, young or old?
Does he drink his soup and his coffee cold,   or HOT,
                                                 The Akond of Swat?

Does he sing or whistle, jabber or talk?
When riding abroad, does he gallop or walk,   or TROT,
                                                 The Akond of Swat?

Does he wear a turban, a fez, or a hat?
Does he sleep on a mattress, a bed, or a mat,   or a COT,
                                                   The Akond of Swat?

When he writes a copy in round-hand size,
Does he cross his t's and finish his i's   with a DOT,
                                              The Akond of Swat?

Can he write a letter concisely clear,
Without a speck or a smudge or smear   or BLOT,
                                          The Akond of Swat?

Do his people like him extremely well?
Or do they, whenever they can, rebel,   or PLOT,
                                           At the Akond of Swat?

If he catches them then, either old or young,
Does he have them chopped in pieces or hung,   or SHOT,
                                                  The Akond of Swat?

Does he study the wants of his own dominion?
Or doesn't he care for public opinion   a JOT,
                                           The Akond of Swat?

To amuse his mind do his people show him
Pictures, or anyone's last new poem,   or WHAT,
                                          The Akond of Swat?

At night if he suddenly screams and wakes,
Do they bring him only a few small cakes,   or a LOT,
                                                    The Akond of Swat?

Does he live on turnips, tea, or tripe?
Does he like his shawl to be marked with a stripe, or a DOT,
                                                    The Akond of Swat?

Is he quiet, or always making a fuss?
Is his steward a Swiss, or a Swede, or a Russ,   or a SCOT,
                                                    The Akond of Swat?

Does he like to sit by the calm blue wave?
Or to sleep and snore in a dark green cave,   or a GROT,
                                                    The Akond of Swat?

Does he drink small beer from a silver jug?
Or a bowl? or a glass? or a cup? or a mug?   or a POT?
                                                    The Akond of Swat?

Does he beat his wife with a gold-topped pipe,
When she lets the gooseberries grow too ripe,   or ROT,
                                                    The Akond of Swat?

Does he wear a white tie when he dines with friends,
And tie it neat in a bow with ends,   or a KNOT,
                                                    The Akond of Swat?

Does he like new cream, and hate mince-pies?
When he looks at the sun does he wink his eyes,   or NOT,
                                                    The Akond of Swat?

Does he teach his subjects to roast and bake?
Does he sail about on an inland lake   in a YACHT,
                                                    The Akond of Swat?

Someone, or nobody, knows I wot
Who, or which, or why, or *what*   Is the Akond of Swat!

EDWARD LEAR

373

THE QUANGLE WANGLE'S HAT

On the top of the Crumpetty Tree
　　The Quangle Wangle sat,
But his face you could not see,
　　On account of his Beaver Hat.
For his Hat was a hundred and two feet wide,
With ribbons and bibbons on every side,
And bells, and buttons, and loops, and lace,
So that nobody ever could see the face
　　Of the Quangle Wangle Quee.

The Quangle Wangle said
　　To himself on the Crumpetty Tree,
"Jam, and jelly, and bread
　　Are the best of food for me!
But the longer I live on this Crumpetty Tree,
The plainer than ever it seems to me
That very few people come this way,
And that life on the whole is far from gay!"
　　Said the Quangle Wangle Quee.

But there came to the Crumpetty Tree
　　Mr. and Mrs. Canary;
And they said, "Did ever you see
　　Any spot so charmingly airy?
May we build a nest on your lovely Hat?
Mr. Quangle Wangle, grant us that!
Oh, please let us come and build a nest
Of whatever material suits you best,
　　Mr. Quangle Wangle Quee!"

And the Golden Grouse came there,
   And the Pobble who has no toes,
And the small Olympian bear,
   And the Dong with a luminous nose.
And the Blue Baboon who played the flute,
And the Orient Calf from the Land of Tute,
And the Attery Squash, and the Bisky Bat—
All came and built on the lovely Hat
   Of the Quangle Wangle Quee.

And the Quangle Wangle said
   To himself on the Crumpetty Tree,
"When all these creatures move
   What a wonderful noise there'll be!"
And at night by the light of the Mulberry moon
They danced to the Flute of the Blue Baboon,
On the broad green leaves of the Crumpetty Tree,
And all were as happy as happy could be,
   With the Quangle Wangle Quee.

EDWARD LEAR

MAD MARGARET'S SONG

From "Ruddigore"

Cherrily carols the lark
  Over the cot.
Merrily whistles the clark
  Scratching a blot.
    But the lark
    And the clark,
    I remark,
  Comfort me not!

Over the ripening peach
  Buzzes the bee.
Splash on the billowy beach
  Tumbles the sea.
    But the peach
    And the beach
    They are each
  Nothing to me!

          W. S. GILBERT

THE KING-FISHER SONG

From "Sylvie and Bruno"

King Fisher courted Lady Bird—
Sing Beans, sing Bones, sing Butterflies!
  "Find me my match," he said,
  "With such a noble head—
With such a beard, as white as curd—
  With such expressive eyes!"

"Yet pins have heads," said Lady Bird—
Sing Prunes, sing Prawns, sing Primrose-Hill!
  "And, where you stick them in,
  They stay, and thus a pin
Is very much to be preferred
  To one that's never still!"

"Oysters have beards," said Lady Bird—
Sing Flies, sing Frogs, sing Fiddle-strings!
  "I love them, for I know
  They never chatter so:
They would not say one single word—
  Not if you crowned them Kings!"

"Needles have eyes," said Lady Bird—
Sing Cats, sing Corks, sing Cowslip-tea!
  "And they are sharp—just what
  Your Majesty is *not:*
So get you gone—'tis too absurd
  To come a-courting *me!*"

LEWIS CARROLL

377

FATHER WILLIAM

From "Alice in Wonderland"

"You are old, Father William," the young man said,
  "And your hair has become very white;
And yet you incessantly stand on your head—
  Do you think at your age, it is right?"

"In my youth," Father William replied to his son,
  "I feared it might injure the brain;
But now that I'm perfectly sure I have none,
  Why, I do it again and again."

"You are old," said the youth, "as I mentioned before,
  And have grown most uncommonly fat;
Yet you turned a back-somersault in at the door—
  Pray, what is the reason for that?"

"In my youth," said the sage, as he shook his gray locks,
  "I kept all my limbs very supple
By the use of this ointment—one shilling the box—
  Allow me to sell you a couple."

"You are old," said the youth, "and your jaws are too weak
  For anything tougher than suet;
Yet you finished the goose, with the bones and the beak;
  Pray, how did you manage to do it?"

"In my youth," said his father, "I took to the law,
  And argued each case with my wife;
And the muscular strength which it gave to my jaw,
  Has lasted the rest of my life."

"You are old," said the youth, "one would hardly suppose
  That your eye was as steady as ever;
Yet you balanced an eel on the end of your nose—
  What made you so awfully clever?"

"I have answered three questions and that is enough,"
  Said the father; "don't give yourself airs!
Do you think I can listen all day to such stuff?
  Be off, or I'll kick you downstairs!"

LEWIS CARROLL

THE WHITE KNIGHT'S TALE

From "Through the Looking-Glass"

"I'll tell thee everything I can:
  There's little to relate.
I saw an agèd, agèd man,
  A-sitting on a gate.
'Who are you, agèd man?' I said.
  'And how is it you live?'
And his answer trickled through my head,
  Like water through a sieve.

"He said, 'I look for butterflies
  That sleep among the wheat:
I make them into mutton-pies,
  And sell them in the street.
I sell them unto men,' he said,
  'Who sail on stormy seas;
And that's the way I get my bread—
  A trifle, if you please.'

"But I was thinking of a plan
     To dye one's whiskers green,
And always use so large a fan
     That they could not be seen.
So, having no reply to give
     To what the old man said,
I cried, 'Come, tell me how you live!'
     And thumped him on the head.

"He said, 'I hunt for haddocks' eyes
     Among the heather bright,
And work them into waistcoat-buttons
     In the silent night.
And these I do not sell for gold
     Or coin of silvery shine,
But for a copper halfpenny,
     And that will purchase nine.'

"I heard him then, for I had just
     Completed my design
To keep the Menai bridge from rust
     By boiling it in wine.
I thanked him much for telling me
     The way he got his wealth,
But chiefly for his wish that he
     Might drink my noble health.

"And now, if e'er by chance I put
     My fingers into glue,
Or madly squeeze a right-hand foot
     Into a left-hand shoe,
Or if I drop upon my toe
     A very heavy weight,
I weep for it reminds me so
     Of that old man I used to know—

Whose look was mild, whose speech was slow,
Whose hair was whiter than the snow,
Whose face was very like a crow,
With eyes, like cinders, all aglow,
Who seemed distracted with his woe,
Who rocked his body to and fro,
And muttered mumblingly and low,
As if his mouth were full of dough,
Who snorted like a buffalo—
That summer evening long ago,
  A-sitting on a gate."

LEWIS CARROLL

JABBERWOCKY

From "Through the Looking-Glass"

'Twas brillig, and the slithy toves
  Did gyre and gimble in the wabe:
All mimsy were the borogoves,
  And the mome raths outgrabe.

"Beware the Jabberwock, my son!
  The jaws that bite, the claws that catch!
Beware the Jubjub bird, and shun
  The frumious Bandersnatch!"

He took his vorpal sword in hand:
  Long time the manxome foe he sought—
So rested he by the Tumtum tree,
  And stood awhile in thought.

And, as in uffish thought he stood,
  The Jabberwock, with eyes of flame,
Came whiffling through the tulgey wood,
  And burbled as it came!

One, two! One, two! And through and through
    The vorpal blade went snicker-snack!
He left it dead, and with its head
    He went galumphing back.

"And hast thou slain the Jabberwock?
    Come to my arms, my beamish boy!
O frabjous day! Callooh! Callay!"
    He chortled in his joy.

'Twas brillig, and the slithy toves
    Did gyre and gimble in the wabe:
All mimsy were the borogoves,
    And the mome raths outgrabe.

LEWIS CARROLL

THE GREAT PANJANDRUM HIMSELF

So she went into the garden
to cut a cabbage-leaf
to make an apple-pie;
and at the same time
a great she-bear, coming down the street,
pops its head into the shop.
What! no soap?
So he died,
and she very imprudently married the Barber.
And there were present
the Picninnies,
and the Joblillies,
and the Garyulies,
and the great Panjandrum himself,
with the little round button at top;
and they all fell to playing the game
of catch-as-catch-can,
till the gunpowder ran out at the heels of their boots.

THE ROAD TO ANYWHERE

THE ROAD TO ANYWHERE

We all love the open road. There is an exciting appeal in the outdoors in spring and autumn; smells and colors are keener; steps are lighter along the highway than on paved streets; the simplest food around a camp-fire of cedar boughs tastes far better than the richest fare in a town restaurant. This appeal may be strongest to those of us who live in houses of stone and steel in modern cities, but even those of us who spend our days in the country enjoy venturing abroad, striding along a new road that may lead to anywhere, meeting new faces, seeing new places—

> A shadowy highway cool and brown,
> Alluring up and enticing down—

happy and carefree with

> An open hand, an easy shoe,
> And a hope to make the day go through.

All men have felt this, though all men have not said so. The poets have said it for them.

> Afoot and light-hearted I take to the open road

sang Walt Whitman almost a hundred years ago.

> Oh, I must up and strike the trail that often I have gone,
> At sunset and at dawn,
> Where all the beauty of the world puts all her splendor on—

echoed Madison Cawein, another American poet, some years later.

More recently poets on both sides of the Atlantic have repeated the sentiment. Bert Leston Taylor, who spent most of his time in a Chicago newspaper office, took up Rudyard Kipling's line from "The Ballad of East and West" and replied:

385

Now east is east, and west is west,
But north lies in between;
And he is blest whose feet have prest
The road that's cool and green.

Gerald Gould, an English poet of our own day, exclaims:

I know not where the white road runs, nor what the blue hills are;
But a man can have the sun for friend, and for his guide a star . . .

John Masefield, the present poet laureate of England, agrees and declares:

It's the white road westwards is the road that I must tread
To the green grass, the cool grass, and rest for heart and head.

And Vachel Lindsay, of Springfield, Illinois, who roamed America on foot, trading his rhymes for bread, always yearned for the free spaces, crying:

I want to go wandering. Who shall declare
I will regret if I dare?

So here, in this section, are poems of caravans which go no one knows where, and of journeys down rivers and through dream-lands, "over the hills and far away . . ." And, finally, there is the little road which strays and stumbles, loafs and loiters, but always leads home.

Perhaps, after all, that is the best road to take.

THE PEDDLER'S CARAVAN

I wish I lived in a caravan,
With a horse to drive, like the peddler-man!
Where he comes from nobody knows,
Or where he goes to, but on he goes!

His caravan has windows two,
And a chimney of tin, that the smoke comes through;
He has a wife, with a baby brown,
And they go riding from town to town.

Chairs to mend, and china to sell!
He clashes the basins like a bell!
Tea-trays, baskets ranged in order,
Plates, with the alphabet round the border!

The roads are brown, and the sea is green,
But his house is just like a bathing-machine;
The world is round, and he can ride,
Rumble and splash, to the other side!

With the peddler-man I should like to roam,
And write a book when I came home;
All the people would read my book,
Just like the Travels of Captain Cook!

WILLIAM BRIGHTY RANDS

OVER THE HILLS AND FAR AWAY

"OVER THE HILLS AND FAR AWAY"

Tom he was a piper's son,
He learned to play when he was young,
But all the tunes that he could play,
Was "Over the hills and far away";

Now Tom with his pipe made such a noise,
That he pleased both girls and boys,
And they stopped to hear him play
"Over the hills and far away."

Tom with his pipe did play with such skill,
That those who heard him could never keep still;
Whenever they heard they began for to dance,
Even pigs on their hind legs would after him prance.

As Dolly was milking her cow one day,
Tom took out his pipe and began for to play;
So Doll and cow danced "The Cheshire Round,"
Till the pail was broke, and the milk ran on the ground.

He met old Dame Trot with a basket of eggs;
He used his pipe, and she used her legs;
She danced about till the eggs were all broke;
She began for to fret, but he laughed at the joke.

He saw a cross fellow was beating an ass,
Heavy laden with pots, pans, dishes, and glass;
He took out his pipe and played them a tune,
And the jackass's load was lightened full soon.

OLD SONG

FAIRY'S WANDER-SONG

Over hill, over dale,
   Thorough [1] bush, thorough brier,
Over park, over pale,
   Thorough flood, thorough fire,
I do wander everywhere,
Swifter than the moonès sphere;
And I serve the fairy queen,
To dew her orbs upon the green.
The cowslips tall her pensioners be;
In their gold coats spots you see,
Those be rubies, fairy favors,
In those freckles live their savors:
I must go seek some dewdrops here,
And hang a pearl in every cowslip's ear.

WILLIAM SHAKESPEARE

MY HEART'S IN THE HIGHLANDS

My heart's in the Highlands, my heart is not here;
My heart's in the Highlands a-chasing the deer;
A-chasing the wild deer, and following the roe—
My heart's in the Highlands wherever I go.

Farewell to the Highlands, farewell to the North,
The birthplace of valor, the country of worth:
Wherever I wander, wherever I rove,
The hills of the Highlands forever I love.

[1] Thorough: through.

Farewell to the mountains high-covered with snow;
Farewell to the straths [1] and green valleys below;
Farewell to the forests and wild-hanging woods;
Farewell to the torrents and loud-pouring floods.

My heart's in the Highlands, my heart is not here,
My heart's in the Highlands a-chasing the deer;
A-chasing the wild deer, and following the roe—
My heart's in the Highlands wherever I go.

ROBERT BURNS

THE FOOTPATH WAY

Jog on, jog on, the footpath way,
    And merrily hent [2] the stile-a;
A merry heart goes all the day,
    Your sad tires in a mile-a.

WILLIAM SHAKESPEARE

THE LAND OF HALLOWE'EN

When October horns are blowing
    And the winds of fall are keen,
And a patch of blue sky's showing
    That the earth is still serene,
Then the sower's done with sowing,
And the mower leaves his mowing,
While each boy and girl is going
    To the land of Hallowe'en.

There the piper's always playing;
    There the lawns are always green;
There's no penalty for straying
    Where the world is just sixteen.

[1] Straths: valleys.

[2] Hent: seize or go over.

Come with laughter and hooraying,
Fling your heels a-holidaying,
For October's gone a-Maying
　To the land of Hallowe'en!

NANCY BIRCKHEAD

WHERE GO THE BOATS?

Dark brown is the river,
　Golden is the sand;
It flows along forever,
　With trees on either hand.

Green leaves a-floating,
　Castles of the foam,
Boats of mine a-boating—
　Where will all come home?

On goes the river
　And out past the mill,
Away down the valley,
　Away down the hill.

Away down the river,
　A hundred miles or more,
Other little children
　Shall bring my boats ashore.

ROBERT LOUIS STEVENSON

FOREIGN LANDS

Up into the cherry tree,
Who should climb but little me?
I held the trunk with both my hands
And looked abroad on foreign lands.

I saw the next-door garden lie,
Adorned with flowers before my eye,
And many pleasant places more
That I had never seen before.

I saw the dimpling river pass
And be the sky's blue looking-glass;
The dusty roads go up and down
With people tramping in to town.

If I could find a higher tree,
Further and further I should see,
To where the grown-up river slips
Into the sea among the ships;

To where the roads on either hand
Lead onward into fairy land,
Where all the children dine at five,
And all the playthings come alive.

ROBERT LOUIS STEVENSON

A PLAN

When I'm a big man, then I'll buy me a gun,
   And a horse and a saddle and whip,
Then I'll jump on his back and give him a whack,
   And away from my mother I'll skip.

Sing hey, sing ho, for a bad little boy,
And away from my mother I'll skip.

I'll gallop and gallop away and away,
   To the place where the Indians live,
And maybe I'll roam, and I'll never come home;
   What a fright to my mother I'll give!

Sing hey, sing ho, for a bad little boy;
What a fright to my mother I'll give.

But then when it's dark, and the wind starts to blow,
    And the ghosts and the gobolings call,
Then I guess if I stayed, that I'd be kind o' 'fraid,
    And I'd want dear mamma after all.

Sing hey, sing ho, for a good little boy,
For I'd want dear mamma after all.

JOHN ALDEN CARPENTER

THE LITTLE ROAD

A little road was straying
    Across a little hill.
I asked, "May I go with you, Road?"
    It answered, "If you will."

'Twas travel-stained and shabby,
    And dust was on its face.
Said I: "How fine to wander free
    To every lovely place!

"O, if you're off to mountains
    Or if you're off to sea,
Or if you're bound across the world,
    It's all the same to me."

We loitered in the sunlight,
    We journeyed on together;
The sky was like a bluebird's wing,
    The wind was like a feather.

We passed a ruddy robin
    Who called, "How do you do?"

Some daisies shook their bonnets back
    And begged, "Ah, take us too!"

A squirrel briefly joined us,
    A brook came hurrying down;
We wandered through a meadow green
    And by a busy town.

    .   .   .   .

When dusky twilight met us,
    No feet so slow as mine.
"Why, there's a little house," I said,
    "With windows all ashine.

"Perhaps, since night is nearing,
    I'd rather rest than roam."
"I knew you would," said Little Road;
    "That's why I brought you home."

NANCY BYRD TURNER

OLD SONGS TO SING

OLD SONGS TO SING

There are times when we want to tell or listen to stories, times when we want to laugh, and there are times when we just want to sing. At such times we want poems with melodies in the lines, or between the lines, poems that almost sing themselves. Sometimes we know the tunes that go with them, sometimes we are tempted to make up the tunes ourselves.

There is this relation between song-poems (sometimes called "lyrics") and nonsense-poems: the music is as important as the meaning of the words—often more important. Every word in the poems in this section is the right word in the right place; and each has been put there, first of all, because of its beauty of sound. Long after we have read the lines we keep on hearing them; they echo in the memory.

You know some of these song-poems, I am sure. You must have heard "On New Year's Day" and "The Nut-Tree" and "Ride a Cock-Horse" ever since you can remember. But don't think any the worse of them for that. The music they make in the mind is real music, as real as "Sally in our Alley," or Tennyson's "A Farewell," or Heywood's spirited "Waking Song," or even Shakespeare's merry "Fairy Song." The same wish to sing that made Cunningham write his rousing "Sea Song" made Blake begin his book with the simplest of happy songs:

> Piping down the valley wild,
> Piping songs of pleasant glee.

Every French boy and girl has delighted in the jolly verses of "The King of Yvetot," but you don't need French to catch the humor and tuneful swing of Thackeray's translation. The words of Burns's "A Red, Red Rose" and Skelton's "Merry Margaret" carry their own music; they almost sing themselves.

But there's little point in explaining such lyrics. A song can be spoilt by talking—during or after the singing. Let us not spoil music by talking too much about it. Let the songs be sung.

ON NEW YEAR'S DAY

I saw three ships come sailing by,
　　Come sailing by, come sailing by;
I saw three ships come sailing by,
　　On New Year's Day in the morning.

And what do you think was in them then,
　　Was in them then, was in them then?
And what do you think was in them then?
　　On New Year's Day in the morning?

Three pretty girls were in them then,
　　Were in them then, were in them then,
Three pretty girls were in them then,
　　On New Year's Day in the morning.

And one could whistle, and one could sing,
　　And one could play on the violin—
Such joy there was at my wedding.
　　On New Year's Day in the morning.

RIDE A COCK-HORSE

Ride a cock-horse to Banbury Cross,
To see an old lady upon a white horse;
Rings on her fingers, and bells on her toes,
She shall have music wherever she goes.

THE NUT-TREE

I had a little nut-tree, nothing would it bear
But a silver nutmeg and a golden pear.

The king of Spain's daughter came to visit me,
And all because of my little nut-tree.

I skipped over water, I danced over sea,
And all the birds in the air couldn't catch me.

MAD FARMER'S SONG

My father he left me three acres of land,
Sing ivy, sing ivy;
My father he left me three acres of land,
Sing holly, go whistle, and ivy!

I plowed it all with a ram's horn,
Sing ivy, sing ivy;
And sowed it all over with one pepper-corn,
Sing holly, go whistle, and ivy!

I harrowed it with a bramble bush,
Sing ivy, sing ivy;
And reaped it with my little penknife,
Sing holly, go whistle, and ivy!

A SONG OF SIXPENCE

Sing a song of sixpence,
A pocket full of rye;
Four and twenty blackbirds
Baked in a pie;

When the pie was opened,
   The birds began to sing;
Wasn't that a dainty dish
   To set before the king?

The king was in his counting-house
   Counting out his money;
The queen was in the parlor
   Eating bread and honey;

The maid was in the garden
   Hanging out the clothes,
Along came a blackbird,
   And nipped off her nose.

SALLY IN OUR ALLEY

Of all the girls that are so smart
   There's none like pretty Sally;
She is the darling of my heart,
   And she lives in our alley.
There is no lady in the land
   Is half so sweet as Sally;
She is the darling of my heart,
   And she lives in our alley.

Her father he makes cabbage-nets
   And through the streets does cry 'em;
Her mother she sells laces long
   To such as please to buy 'em:
But sure such folks could ne'er beget
   So sweet a girl as Sally!
She is the darling of my heart,
   And she lives in our alley.

Of all the days that's in the week
    I dearly love but one day—
And that's the day that comes betwixt
    A Saturday and Monday;
For then I'm drest all in my best
    To walk abroad with Sally;
She is the darling of my heart,
    And she lives in our alley.

                              HENRY CAREY

THE KING OF YVETOT

There was a king of Yvetot,
    Of whom renown hath little said,
Who let all thoughts of glory go,
    And dawdled half his days a-bed;
And every night, as night came round,
By Jenny, with a nightcap crowned,
    Slept very sound.
    Sing ho, ho, ho! and he, he, he!
    That's the kind of king for me.

And every day it came to pass
    That four lusty meals made he;
And, step by step, upon an ass,
    Rode abroad, his realms to see;
And wherever he did stir,
What think you was his escort, sir?
    Why, an old cur.
    Sing ho, ho, ho! and he, he, he!
    That's the kind of king for me.

To all the ladies of the land,
    A courteous king, and kind, was he;

The reason why you'll understand,
    They named him *Pater Patriae.*[1]
Each year he called his fighting men
And marched a league from home, and then
    Marched back again.
    Sing ho, ho, ho! and he, he, he!
    That's the kind of king for me.

The portrait of this best of kings
    Is standing still, upon a sign
That on a village tavern swings,
    Famed in the country for good wine.
The people in their Sunday trim,
Filling their glasses to the brim,
    Look up to him,
    Singing ho, ho, ho! and he, he, he!
    That's the kind of king for me.

                    After the French of BERANGER
                    Adapted by William Makepeace Thackeray

THE MINARET BELLS

Tink-a-tink, tink-a-tink,
    By the light of the star,
On the blue river's brink,
    I heard a guitar.

I heard a guitar,
    On the blue waters clear,
And knew by its music
    That Selim was near!

Tink-a-tink, tink-a-tink,
    How the soft music swells,

[1] *Pater Patriae:* Father of his country.

And I hear the soft clink
Of the minaret bells!

WILLIAM MAKEPEACE THACKERAY

MERRY MARGARET

Merry Margaret,
As midsummer flower,
Gentle as falcon,
Or hawk of the tower;
With solace and gladness,
Much mirth and no madness,
All good and no badness;
So joyously,
So maidenly,
So womanly,
Her demeaning,
In everything,
Far, far passing
That I can indite,
Or suffice to write,
Of merry Margaret,
As midsummer flower,
Gentle as falcon,
Or hawk of the tower;
As patient and as still,
And as full of goodwill,
As fair Isiphil,
Coliander,
Sweet Pomander,
Good Cassander;
Stedfast of thought,

Well made, well wrought,
Far may be sought,
Ere you can find
So courteous, so kind,
As merry Margaret,
This midsummer flower,
Gentle as falcon,
Or hawk of the tower.

JOHN SKELTON

A RED, RED ROSE

O, my luve is like a red, red rose,
   That's newly sprung in June.
O, my luve is like the melodie
   That's sweetly play'd in tune.

As fair art thou, my bonnie lass,
   So deep in luve am I,
And I will luve thee still, my dear,
   Till a' the seas gang dry.

Till a' the seas gang dry, my dear,
   And the rocks melt wi' the sun!
And I will luve thee still, my dear,
   While the sands o' life shall run.

And fare thee weel, my only luve,
   And fare thee weel a while!
And I will come again, my luve,
   Tho' it were ten thousand mile!

ROBERT BURNS

BRIAR-ROSE

Once a boy espied a rose,
   Rose-upon-the-briar,
Radiant as a cloud that glows;
So he ran to see it close,
   Saw it with desire.
Rosebud, rosebud, lovely rose,
   Rose-upon-the-briar.

"I will cut you short," said he,
   Rose-upon-the-briar."
Rose said, "Better let me be,
Or I'll make you think of me
   And my thorn of fire."
Rosebud, rosebud, lovely rose,
   Rose-upon-the-briar.

Then he raised his hand to break
   Rose-upon-the-briar,
Stopping not for pity's sake,
Till he felt the fiery ache
   Burning hot and higher.
Rosebud, rosebud, lovely rose,
   Rose-upon-the-briar.

GERMAN FOLK-SONG
Adapted by Louis Untermeyer

TO GLOW-WORMS

Ye living lamps, by whose dear light
The nightingale does sit so late,
And, studying all the summer night,
Her matchless songs does meditate;

Ye country comets, that portend
No war nor prince's funeral,
Shining unto no higher end
Than to presage the grass's fall;

Ye glow-worms, whose officious flame
To wandering mowers shows the way,
That in the night have lost their aim
And after foolish fires do stray;

Your courteous lights in vain you waste,
Since Juliana here is come,
For she my mind hath so displaced,
That I shall never find my home.

ANDREW MARVELL

A FAREWELL

Flow down, cold rivulet, to the sea,
  Thy tribute wave deliver:
No more by thee my steps shall be,
  For ever and for ever.

Flow, softly flow, by lawn and lea,
    A rivulet, then a river:
No where by thee my steps shall be,
    For ever and for ever.

But here will sigh thine alder tree,
    And here thine aspen shiver;
And here by thee will hum the bee,
    For ever and for ever.

ALFRED, LORD TENNYSON

WAKING SONG

Pack, clouds, away! and welcome, day!
    With night we banish sorrow.
Sweet air, blow soft; mount, lark, aloft
    To give my Love good-morrow.
Wings from the wind to please her mind,
    Notes from the lark I'll borrow:
Bird, prune thy wing! nightingale, sing,
    To give my Love good-morrow!
    To give my Love good-morrow
    Notes from them all I'll borrow.

Wake from thy nest, robin red-breast!
    Sing, birds, in every furrow.
And from each bill let music shrill
    Give my fair Love good-morrow.
Blackbird and thrush in every bush,
    Stare, linnet, and cock-sparrow,
You pretty elves, amongst yourselves,
    Sing my fair Love good-morrow!
    To give my Love good-morrow
    Sing, birds, in every furrow!

THOMAS HEYWOOD

A SEA SONG

A wet sheet and a flowing sea,
  A wind that follows fast
And fills the white and rustling sail
  And bends the gallant mast;
And bends the gallant mast, my boys,
  While like the eagle free
Away the good ship flies, and leaves
  Old England on the lee.

O for a soft and gentle wind!
  I heard a fair one cry;
But give to me the snoring breeze
  And white waves heaving high;
And white waves heaving high, my lads,
  The good ship tight and free—
The world of waters is our home,
  And merry men are we.

There's tempest in yon hornéd moon,
  And lightning in yon cloud;
But hark the music, mariners!
  The wind is piping loud;
The wind is piping loud, my boys,
  The lightning flashes free—
While the hollow oak our palace is,
  Our heritage the sea.

                    ALLAN CUNNINGHAM

FAIRY SONG

Where the bee sucks, there suck I:
In a cowslip's bell I lie;
There I couch when owls do cry.
On the bat's back I do fly
After summer merrily:
Merrily, merrily shall I live now
Under the blossom that hangs on the bough.

WILLIAM SHAKESPEARE

HAPPY SONGS

Piping down the valleys wild,
Piping songs of pleasant glee,
On a cloud I saw a child,
And he laughing said to me:

"Pipe a song about a Lamb!"
So I piped with merry cheer.
"Piper, pipe that song again;"
So I piped: he wept to hear.

"Drop thy pipe, thy happy pipe,
Sing thy songs of happy cheer."
So I sung the same again
While he wept with joy to hear.

"Piper, sit thee down and write
In a book that all may read."
So he vanish'd from my sight,
And I pluck'd a hollow reed,

And I made a rural pen,
And I stain'd the water clear,
And I wrote my happy songs
Every child may joy to hear.

WILLIAM BLAKE

HUSH-A-BY

HUSH-A-BY

Lullabies are, probably, the oldest kind of poetry in the world. Long before men thought of writing poems on paper, even before priests chanted in front of altars or tribesmen danced around camp-fires, mothers rocked their babes to sleep and murmured a few soothing sounds. These sounds became words, the words grew into sentences, the sentences shaped themselves into verse, and the lullaby was born. Soon the world was full of slumber-songs. And the savage mother, hushing her baby at her breast, crooned much the same sort of thing as the queen-mother, quieting her babe in the royal cradle.

That is why the lullabies in this section are not so different from each other. England and Italy are not at all alike, Germany and Spain have not much in common; but there is little difference between English, Italian, German and Spanish babes. Mothers in all countries have a way of promising the little ones great things if they will only go to sleep, telling them how famous they will become and how proud their mothers will be, or threatening them—all in the same lulling tones.

Here you have lullabies from almost every country—even from Fairyland. Some are so old that no one has a record of them; some are as new as yesterday. Some have been sung to little home-made melodies; some have been put to music by the great composers—both Brahms and Schumann have set the songs about the Sandman.

Lastly there is William Blake's "Cradle Song." As far as I know, no composer has ever written music for these hushed and holy lines. No one needs to. They make their own music.

OLD ENGLISH SLUMBER SONGS

Matthew, Mark, Luke, and John,
Guard the bed that I lie on.
Four corners to my bed;
Four angels round my head,
One to watch, one to pray,
And two to bear my soul away.

By, baby bunting,
Daddy's gone a-hunting,
To get a little rabbit skin
To wrap my baby bunting in.

Hush-a-by, baby, on the tree-top;
When the wind blows, the cradle will rock;
When the bough breaks, the cradle will fall;
Down will come baby, bough, cradle, and all.

Dance to your daddy,
My little babby,
Dance to your daddy,
My little lamb.

You shall have a fishy,
In a little dishy,
You shall have a fishy
When the boat comes in.

Rock-a-by, baby, thy cradle is green;
Father's a nobleman, mother's a queen;
Betty's a lady, and wears a gold ring;
And Johnny's a drummer, and drums for the King.

ROMAN LULLABY

Lie low; my little one
Shall have all that's nice:
Alexandria for sugar,
Cairo for rice.

Constantinople
Will give you its treasure;
The bells of Saint Peter
Will ring for your pleasure.
Adapted by L. U.

OLD GERMAN LULLABIES

I.

Sleep, baby, sleep,
Thy father herds the sheep;
Thy mother's here and tends the geese;
So sleep, my babe, and take thy peace.
Sleep, baby, sleep.

2.

Sleep, this is the time for sleep.
In the garden there walk two sheep.
One is black and one is white;
The little black one waits to bite
Any child who starts to weep.
So sleep, darling, sleep.
Adapted by L. U.

SARDINIAN LULLABY

Oh! ninna and anninia!
  Sleep, baby boy;
Oh! ninna and anninia!
  God give thee joy.
Oh! ninna and anninia!
  Sweet joy be thine;
Oh! ninna and anninia!
  Sleep, brother mine.

JEWISH LULLABY

Husha, oh, husha
  And lull-lullaby,
No mother in Russia
  Is prouder than I.
You stumble no longer,
  Soon you will run,
And you will grow stronger
  Than Samson, my son.

Husha, oh, husha
  And lull-lullaby.

You will grow famous;
  Your thoughts will go wide.
Isaiah and Amos
  Will walk by your side.

Your words will be graven
On metal and stone,
And the great ones in Heaven
Will envy my son.

*Husha, oh, husha,
And lull-lullaby.*

LOUIS UNTERMEYER

SPANISH LULLABY

The poor Son of Mary,
Cradle He had none;
His father was a carpenter,
So he made Him one.

His father made a cradle
Of wood he had found;
Mary Mother rocked Him,
And then He slept sound.

You, too, sleep, my baby,
Never you fear;
Mother is beside you,
The Son of God is near.

Adapted by L. U.

FAIRY LULLABY

From "A Midsummer Night's Dream"

First Fairy

You spotted snakes with double tongue,
 Thorny hedgehogs be not seen;
Newts, and blind-worms, do no wrong;
 Come not near our fairy queen.

Chorus

Philomel with melody
 Sing in our sweet lullaby;
Lulla, lulla, lullaby; lulla, lulla, lullaby!
Never harm, nor spell, nor charm,
 Come our lovely lady nigh!
 So good-night, with lullaby.

Second Fairy

Weaving spiders, come not here;
 Hence, you long-legged spinners, hence;
Beetles black, approach not near;
 Worm, nor snail, do no offense.

425

PHILOMEL WITH MELODY

Chorus

Philomel with melody
Sing in our sweet lullaby;
Lulla, lulla, lullaby; lulla, lulla, lullaby!
Never harm, nor spell, nor charm,
Come our lovely lady nigh!
So good-night, with lullaby.

WILLIAM SHAKESPEARE

LULLABY

Lullaby, oh, lullaby!
Flowers are closed and lambs are sleeping;
Lullaby, oh, lullaby!
Stars are up, the moon is peeping;
Lullaby, oh, lullaby!
While the birds are silence keeping,
Lullaby, oh, lullaby!
Sleep, my baby, fall a-sleeping,
Lullaby, oh, lullaby!

CHRISTINA ROSSETTI

LULLABY OF AN INFANT CHIEF

Oh, hush thee, my baby, thy sire was a knight,
Thy mother a lady, both lovely and bright;
The woods and the glens, from the towers we see,
They all are belonging, dear baby, to thee.

Oh, fear not the bugle, though loudly it blows,
It calls but the warders that guard thy repose;
Their bows would be bended, their blades would be red,
Ere the step of a foeman draws near to thy bed.

Oh, hush thee, my baby, the time will soon come
When thy sleep shall be broken by trumpet and drum;
Then hush thee, my darling, take rest while you may,
For strife comes with manhood, and waking with day.

WALTER SCOTT

OLD DADDY DARKNESS

Old Daddy Darkness creeps from his hole,
Black as a blackamoor, blind as a mole;
Stir the fire till it glows, let the little ones sit,
Old Daddy Darkness is not wanted yet. . . .

Close your eyes, then you will see Daddy best;
He's in below the bed-clothes, to cuddle you to rest.
Now nestle in his bosom, sleep, and dream your fill,
Till Wee Davie Daylight comes peepin' o'er the hill.

Adapted from the Scotch of James Ferguson

THE ROCK-A-BY LADY

The Rock-a-By Lady from Hushaby Street
   Comes stealing; comes creeping;
The poppies they hang from her head to her feet,
And each hath a dream that is tiny and fleet—
She bringeth her poppies to you, my sweet,
   When she findeth you sleeping!

There is one little dream of a beautiful drum—
   "Rub-a-dub!" it goeth;
There is one little dream of a big sugar-plum,
And lo! thick and fast the other dreams come
Of popguns that bang, and tin tops that hum,
   And a trumpet that bloweth!

And dollies peep out of those wee little dreams
   With laughter and singing;
And boats go a-floating on silvery streams,
And the stars peek-a-boo with their own misty gleams,
And up, up, and up, where the Mother Moon beams,
   The fairies go winging!

Would you dream all these dreams that are tiny and fleet?
   They'll come to you sleeping;
So shut the two eyes that are weary, my sweet,
For the Rock-a-By Lady from Hushaby Street,
With poppies that hang from her head to her feet,
   Comes stealing; comes creeping.

EUGENE FIELD

GO TO SLEEP

Go to sleep and good night;
In a rosy twilight,
With the moon overhead
Snuggle deep in your bed.
God will watch, never fear,
While Heaven draws near.

Go to sleep and good night;
You are safe in the sight
Of the angels who show
Christmas trees all aglow.
So to sleep, shut your eyes,
In a dream's Paradise.

From the German of KARL SIMROCK
Adapted by L. U.

THE SANDMAN

I have a pair of boots so rare
They carry me as light as air,
And, with the bag of sand I've brought,
Run up the stairs as quick as thought.
And there within the room I see
The children praying sleepily.
Two grains of sea-sand, fairy-wise,
I lay upon their tired eyes
To give them dreams of long delight
While angels guard them through the night.

Two grains of sea-sand fairy-wise,
I lay upon their tired eyes,
And happy dreams it's understood
Will come to every child that's good.
Then in a flash I leave them there
And hurry, hurry, down the stair.
I cannot stop for I must be
Where other children wait for me.
And, as I glide on starry beams,
I leave them all in laughing dreams.

From the German
Adapted by L. U.

LITTLE SANDMAN'S SONG

The flowers all are sleeping
  Safe in their starlit beds,
And as the moon comes creeping
  They nod their fragrant heads.
The drowsy, budding branch lets fall
An air that seems to call:
  Sleep a while, sleep a while,
  My children, sleep a while.

The birds that sang so bravely
  Are silent in the nest;
The sun itself has gravely
  Found pillows in the west.
The cricket as he grinds away
Works all night long to say:
  Sleep a while, sleep a while,
  My children, sleep a while.

The Sandman comes in gliding
  Up to each sleepyhead
To see if someone's hiding
  Who should have gone to bed.
And when a yawning child he spies,
He drops sand in his eyes.
  Sleep a while, sleep a while,
  My children, sleep a while.

From the German
Adapted by L. U.

A CRADLE SONG

Sweet dreams, form a shade
O'er my lovely infant's head;
Sweet dreams of pleasant streams
By happy, silent, moony beams.

Sweet sleep, with soft down
Weave thy brows an infant crown,
Sweet sleep, Angel mild,
Hover o'er my happy child.

Sweet smiles, in the night
Hover over my delight;
Sweet smiles, mother's smiles,
All the livelong night beguiles.

Sweet moans, dovelike sighs,
Chase not slumber from thy eyes.
Sweet moans, sweeter smiles,
All the dovelike moans beguiles.

Sleep, sleep, happy child,
All creation slept and smiled;
Sleep, sleep, happy sleep,
While o'er thee thy mother weep.

Sweet babe, in thy face
Holy image I can trace.
Sweet babe, once like thee,
Thy Maker lay and wept for me,

Wept for me, for thee, for all,
When He was an infant small.
Thou His image ever see,
Heavenly face that smiles on thee,

Smiles on thee, on me, on all;
Who became an infant small.
Infant smiles are His own smiles;
Heaven and earth to peace beguiles.

WILLIAM BLAKE

DAY'S END

Night is come,
  Owls are out;
Beetles hum
  Round about.

Children snore
  Safe in bed;
Nothing more
  Need be said.

HENRY NEWBOLT

TRUE ARROWS

TRUE ARROWS

There are many ways of teaching a lesson, but there is none that goes so straight to the mark as a story. That is why speakers begin their speeches and preachers weave into their sermons stories that are swift and pointed. And that is why I have called them "true arrows."

These feathered poems fly swiftly to their mark. Some of them are legends, others are fables, still others are little proverbs and sayings—but all carry a keen something to "point a moral or adorn a tale." Phoebe Cary's "A Legend of the Northland" was once very popular although now it is almost forgotten. I have left out a few of the verses so that the arrow might fly swifter—in this case the arrow hits the target of selfishness. See, says the poet, what happened to a woman who was too selfish to give a tiny scrap of dough to a hungry saint.

"The Spider and the Fly" is a fable, and a famous one, that teaches us not to be vain and to pay no attention to silly, flattering words. "The Butterfly and the Caterpillar" tells us not to be proud of position, looks, or fine clothes. "The Fox and the Grapes" shows that we shouldn't desire what we cannot get, and "The Frogs Who Wanted a King" shows we should be satisfied with what we have. "The Bee, the Ant, and the Sparrow" shows that if you are cruel to others, someone will be cruel to you. "The Priest and the Mulberry Tree" teaches that it's not wise to say everything we happen to think.

"Abou Ben Adhem" shows the beauty of being modest. So, in another way, does "The Violet." "Climbing to the Light" counsels us never to give up. "Eldorado" declares that anything worth finding and winning is worth hard searching, even though mountains have to be mounted and long valleys spanned:

> "Ride, boldly ride"
> The shade replied,
> "If you seek for Eldorado!"

437

"Vegetable Fantasies" and the "Proverbs," which I found in Germany, need no further words from me. Neither do the other poems.

It is with a rainbow that this book began, and it is with a rainbow that it ends.

A LEGEND OF THE NORTHLAND

Away, away in the Northland,
   Where the hours of day are few,
And the nights are so long in winter
   That they cannot sleep them through;

Where they harness the swift reindeer
   To the sledges when it snows;
And the children look like bear's cubs
   In their funny, furry clothes:

They tell them a curious story—
   I don't believe 'tis true;
And yet you may learn a lesson
   If I tell the tale to you.

Once, when the good Saint Peter
   Lived in the world below,
And walked about it, preaching,
   Just as he did, you know,

He came to the door of a cottage,
   In traveling round the earth,
Where a little woman was making cakes,
   And baking them on the hearth;

And being faint with fasting,
   For the day was almost done,
He asked her, from her store of cakes,
   To give him a single one.

So she made a very little cake,
    But as it baking lay,
She looked at it, and thought it seemed
    Too large to give away.

Therefore she kneaded another,
    And still a smaller one;
But it looked, when she turned it over,
    As large as the first had done.

Then she took a tiny scrap of dough,
    And rolled and rolled it flat;
And baked it thin as a wafer—
    But she couldn't part with that.

For she said, "My cakes that seem too small
    When I eat of them myself,
Are yet too large to give away."
    So she put them on the shelf.

Then good Saint Peter grew angry,
    For he was hungry and faint;
And surely such a woman
    Was enough to provoke a saint.

And he said, "You are far too selfish
    To dwell in a human form,
To have both food and shelter,
    And fire to keep you warm.

"Now, you shall build as the birds do,
    And shall get your scanty food
By boring, and boring, and boring,
    All day in the hard dry wood."

Then up she went through the chimney,
    Never speaking a word,
And out of the top flew a woodpecker,
    For she was changed to a bird.

She had a scarlet cap on her head,
    And that was left the same,
But all the rest of her clothes were burned
    Black as a coal in the flame.

And every country schoolboy
    Has seen her in the wood,
Where she lives in the trees till this very day,
    Boring and boring for food.

PHOEBE CARY

THE SPIDER AND THE FLY

A Fable

"Will you walk into my parlor?" said the spider to the fly;
" 'Tis the prettiest little parlor that ever you did spy.
The way into my parlor is up a winding stair,
And I have many pretty things to show when you are there."
"O no, no," said the little fly, "to ask me is in vain,
For who goes up your winding stair can ne'er come down again."

Said the cunning spider to the fly, "Dear friend, what shall I do,
To prove the warm affection I've always felt for you?
I have within my pantry good store of all that's nice;
I'm sure you're very welcome; will you please to take a slice?"
"O no, no," said the little fly, "kind sir, that cannot be;
I've heard what's in your pantry, and I do not wish to see."

The spider turned him round about, and went into his den,
For well he knew the silly fly would soon be back again:
So he wove a subtle web in a little corner sly,
And set his table ready to dine upon the fly.
Then he came out to his door again, and merrily did sing,
"Come hither, hither, pretty fly, with the pearl and silver wing:
Your robes are green and purple; there's a crest upon your head;
Your eyes are like the diamond bright, but mine are dull as lead."

Alas, alas! How very soon this silly little fly,
Hearing his wily flattering words, came slowly flitting by.
With buzzing wings she hung aloft, then near and nearer drew,
Thinking only of her brilliant eyes, and green and purple hue;
Thinking only of her crested head—*poor foolish thing!* At last
Up jumped the cunning spider, and fiercely held her fast.
He dragged her up his winding stair, into his dismal den,
Within his little parlor; but she ne'er came out again!

And now, dear little children, who may this story read,
To idle, silly, flattering words, I pray you ne'er give heed;
Unto an evil counselor close heart, and ear, and eye,
And take a lesson from this tale of the Spider and the Fly.

MARY HOWITT

CLIMBING TO THE LIGHT

The ivy in the dungeon grew,
Unfed by rain, uncheered by dew;
Its pallid leaflets only drank
Cave-moisture foul, and odors rank.

But through the dungeon's grating high,
There fell a sunbeam from the sky;
It slept upon the grateful floor,
In silent gladness evermore.

The ivy felt a tremor shoot
Through all its fibers to the root;
It felt the light, it saw the ray,
And strove to blossom into day.

It grew, it crept, it pushed, it clomb,[1]
Long had the darkness been its home;
But well it knew, though veiled in night,
The goodness and the joy of light.

Its clinging roots grew deep and strong,
Its stem expanded prim and long,
And in the currents of the air
Its tender branches flourished fair.

It reached the beam, it thrilled, it curled,
It blessed the warmth that cheers the world;
It rose up to the dungeon-bars,
And gazed upon the sun and stars.

By rains, and dews, and sunshine fed,
Over the outer walls it spread;
And in the day-beam waving free,
It grew into a steadfast tree.

Wouldst know the moral of the rhyme?
Behold the heavenly light and climb:
To every dungeon comes some ray
Of God's interminable day.

CHARLES MACKAY

[1] Clomb: climbed.

THE BUTTERFLY AND THE CATERPILLAR [1]

A Fable Old Is Here Retold

A butterfly, one summer morn,
Sat on a spray of blossoming thorn
And, as he sipped and drank his share
Of honey from the flowered air,
Below, upon the garden wall,
A caterpillar chanced to crawl.
"Horrors!" the butterfly exclaimed,
"This must be stopped! I am ashamed
That such as I should have to be
In the same world with such as he.
Preserve me from such hideous things!
Disgusting shape! Where are his wings!
Fuzzy and gray! Eater of clay!
Won't someone take the worm away!"

The caterpillar crawled ahead,
But, as he munched a leaf, he said,
"Eight days ago, young butterfly,
You wormed about, the same as I;
Within a fortnight from today
Two wings will bear me far away,
To brighter blooms and lovelier lures,
With colors that outrival yours.

[1] If you would like to see how another poet has written about these two creatures—in a quite different way—turn to page 248.

So, flutter-flit, be not so proud;
Each caterpillar is endowed
With power to make him by and by,
A blithe and brilliant butterfly.
While you, who scorn the common clay,
You, in your livery so gay,
And all the gaudy moths and millers,
Are only dressed-up caterpillars."

JOSEPH LAUREN

THE FOX AND THE GRAPES

A Moral Tale for Those Who Fail

One summer's day a Fox was passing through
An orchard; faint he was and hungry, too.
When suddenly his keen eye chanced to fall
Upon a bunch of grapes above the wall.

"Ha! Just the thing!" he said. "Who could resist it!"
He eyed the purple cluster—jumped—and missed it.
"Ahem!" he coughed. "I'll take more careful aim,"
And sprang again. Results were much the same,
Although his leaps were desperate and high.
At length he paused to wipe a tearful eye,
And shrug a shoulder. "I am not so dry,
And lunch is bound to come within the hour . . .
Besides," he said, "I'm sure those grapes are sour."

THE MORAL is: We somehow want the peach
That always dangles just beyond our reach;
Until we learn never to be upset
With what we find too difficult to get.

JOSEPH LAUREN

THE FROGS WHO WANTED A KING

The frogs were living happy as could be
    In a wet marsh to which they all were suited;
From every sort of trouble they were free,
    And all night long they croaked, and honked, and hooted.
But one fine day a bull-frog said, "The thing
We never had and *must* have is a king."

So all the frogs immediately prayed;
    "Great Jove," they chorused from their swampy border,
"Send us a king and he will be obeyed,
    A king to bring a rule of Law and Order."
Jove heard and chuckled. That night in the bog
There fell a long and most impressive Log.

The swamp was silent; nothing breathed. At first
    The badly frightened frogs did never *once* stir;
But gradually some neared and even durst
    To touch, aye, even dance upon, the monster.
Whereat they croaked again, "Great Jove, oh hear!
Send us a *living* king, a king to fear."

Once more Jove smiled, and sent them down a Stork.
    "Long live—!" they croaked. But ere they framed the sentence,
The Stork bent down and, scorning knife or fork,
    Swallowed them all, with no time for repentance!

THE MORAL'S this: No matter what your lot,
It might be worse. Be glad with what you've got.

JOSEPH LAUREN

THE NIGHTINGALE AND THE GLOW-WORM

A Nightingale that all day long
Had cheered the village with his song,
Nor yet at eve his note suspended,
Nor yet when eventide was ended,
Began to feel, as well he might,
The keen demands of appetite;
When looking eagerly around,
He spied far off, upon the ground,
A something shining in the dark,
And knew the Glow-worm by his spark;
So, stooping down from hawthorn top,
He thought to put him in his crop.
The worm, aware of his intent,
Harangued him thus, right eloquent:
"Did you admire my lamp," quoth he,
"As much as I your minstrelsy,
You would abhor to do me wrong,
As much as I to spoil your song:
For 'twas the self-same Power Divine
Taught you to sing and me to shine,
That you with music, I with light,
Might beautify and cheer the night."
The songster heard this short oration,
And warbling out his approbation,
Released him, as my story tells,
And found a supper somewhere else.

WILLIAM COWPER

447

THE BEE, THE ANT, AND THE SPARROW

My dears, 'tis said in days of old
That beasts could talk, and birds could scold:
There met a Sparrow, Ant, and Bee,
Which reasoned and conversed as we.
—Now to my tale: One summer's dawn
A Bee ranged o'er the verdant lawn;
Studious to husband every hour,
And make the most of every flower.
Nimble from stalk to stalk she flies,
And loads with yellow wax her thighs;
With which the artist builds her comb,
And keeps all tight and warm at home;
Or from the cowslip's golden bells
Sucks honey to enrich her cells:
Or every tempting rose pursues,
Or sips the lily's fragrant dews;
Yet never robs the shining bloom,
Or of its beauty or perfume.
Thus she discharged in every way
The various duties of the day.

It chanced a frugal Ant was near,
Whose brow was wrinkled o'er by care;
A great economist was she,
Nor less laborious than the Bee.

The active Bee with pleasure saw
The Ant fulfill her parent's law.

"Ah! sister laborer," says she,
"How very fortunate are we!
Who, taught in infancy to know
The comforts which from labor flow.
Why is our food so very sweet?
Because we earn before we eat.
Why are our wants so very few?
Because we Nature's call pursue.
Have we incessant tasks to do?
Is not all Nature busy too?
Doth not the sun, with constant pace,
Persist to run his annual race?
Do not the stars which shine so bright,
Renew their courses every night?
Doth not the ox obedient bow
His patient neck, and draw the plow?"

A wanton Sparrow longed to hear
Their sage discourse, and straight drew near,
The bird was talkative and loud,
And very pert and very proud;
As worthless and as vain a thing,
Perhaps, as ever wore a wing.
She found, as on a spray she sat,
The little friends were deep in chat.

She viewed the Ant with savage eyes,
And hopped and hopped to snatch the prize.
The Bee, who watched her opening bill,
And guessed her fell design to kill,
Asked her from what her anger rose,
And why she treated Ants as foes?

The Sparrow her reply began,
And thus the conversation ran:

"Whenever I'm disposed to dine,
I think the whole creation mine;
That I'm a bird of high degree,
And every insect made for me.
Hence oft I search the emmet-brood [1]
(For emmets are delicious food),
And oft, in wantonness and play,
I slay ten thousand in a day.
For truth it is, without disguise,
That I love mischief as my eyes."

A prowling cat the miscreant spies,
And wide expands her amber eyes:
Near and more near Grimalkin [2] draws;
She wags her tail, extends her paws;
Then, springing on her thoughtless prey,
She bore the vicious bird away.

Thus in her cruelty and pride,
The wicked, wanton sparrow died.

CHARLES COTTON

THE PRIEST AND THE MULBERRY-TREE

Did you hear of the curate who mounted his mare,
And merrily trotted along to the fair?
Of creature more tractable none ever heard,
At the height of her speed she would stop at a word;
But again with a word, when the curate said, *Hey!*
She put forth her mettle and galloped away.

[1] Emmet: ant.   [2] Grimalkin: the cat.

As near to the gates of the city he rode,
While the sun of September all brilliantly glowed,
The good priest discovered, with eyes of desire,
A mulberry-tree in a hedge of wild briar;
On boughs long and lofty, in many a green shoot,
Hung large, black, and glossy, the beautiful fruit.

The curate was hungry and thirsty to boot;
He shrunk from the thorns, though he longed for the fruit;
With a word he arrested his courser's keen speed,
And he stood up erect on the back of his steed;
On the saddle he stood while the creature stood still,
And he gathered the fruit till he took his good fill.

"Sure never," he thought, "was a creature so rare,
So docile, so true, as my excellent mare;
Lo, here now I stand," and he gazed all around,
"As safe and as steady as if on the ground.
Yet how had it been, if some traveler this way,
Had, dreaming no mischief, but chanced to cry, *Hey!*"

He stood with his head in the mulberry-tree,
And he spoke out aloud in his fond reverie.
At the sound of the word the good mare made a push,
And down went the priest in the wild-briar bush!
He remembered too late, on his thorny green bed,
Much that well may be thought cannot wisely be said.

THOMAS LOVE PEACOCK

451

RULES FOR THE ROAD

Stand straight:
Step firmly, throw your weight:
The heaven is high above your head,
The good gray road is faithful to your tread.

Be strong:
Sing to your heart a battle song:
Though hidden foemen lie in wait,
Something is in you that can smile at Fate.

Press through:
Nothing can harm if you are true.
And when the night comes, rest:
The earth is friendly as a mother's breast.

EDWIN MARKHAM

BEN ADHEM'S NAME LED ALL THE REST

ABOU BEN ADHEM

Abou Ben Adhem (may his tribe increase!)
Awoke one night from a deep dream of peace,
And saw within the moonlight in his room,
Making it rich and like a lily in bloom,
An angel writing in a book of gold:
Exceeding peace had made Ben Adhem bold,
And to the presence in the room he said,
"What writest thou?" The vision raised its head,
And, with a look made of all sweet accord,
Answered, "The names of those who love the Lord."
"And is mine one?" said Abou. "Nay, not so,"
Replied the angel. Abou spoke more low,
But cheerily still; and said, "I pray thee, then,
Write me as one that loves his fellow-men."

The angel wrote, and vanished. The next night
It came again, with a great wakening light,
And showed the names whom love of God had blessed,—
And, lo! Ben Adhem's name led all the rest!

LEIGH HUNT

ELDORADO

Gayly bedight,
A gallant knight,
In sunshine and in shadow,
Had journeyed long,
Singing a song,
In search of Eldorado.

But he grew old—
This knight so bold—
And o'er his heart a shadow
Fell as he found
No spot of ground
That looked like Eldorado.

And, as his strength
Failed him at length,
He met a pilgrim shadow.
"Shadow," said he,
"Where can it be—
This land of Eldorado?"

"Over the Mountains
Of the Moon,
Down the Valley of the Shadow,
Ride, boldly ride,"
The shade replied,
"If you seek for Eldorado!"

EDGAR ALLAN POE

COUNTRY SAYING

He that would thrive,
Must rise at five;
He that hath thriven
May lie till seven;
And he that by the plow would thrive,
Himself must either hold or drive.

A LESSON

A Toadstool comes up in a night,—
   Learn the lesson, little folk:
An oak grows on a hundred years,
   But then it is an oak.

          CHRISTINA ROSSETTI

THE VIOLET

Down in a green and shady bed
   A modest violet grew;
Its stalk was bent, it hung its head,
   As if to hide from view.

And yet it was a lovely flower,
   Its color bright and fair!
It might have graced a rosy bower,
   Instead of hiding there.

Yet there it was content to bloom,
   In modest tints arrayed;
And there diffused its sweet perfume
   Within the silent shade.

Then let me to the valley go,
   This pretty flower to see,
That I may also learn to grow
   In sweet humility.

          JANE TAYLOR

VEGETABLE FANTASIES

Oscar was a radish
Blond and tall and slim,
All the lady radishes
Flirted with him.

He was so proud
He grew above them all;
But the gardener pulled him
Because he was too tall.

The moral is here:
Don't be too high,
Or you'll get weeded out
By and by.

Prissie was a turnip,
One of the élite,
Long were her fingers
And slender her feet.

Where now is Prissie,
Say, can you tell?
Boiled in the dinner,
Which tastes very well.

Hugh was a cabbage
Sturdy and strong,
Who sat in the garden
Singing a song.

He was so noisy
The cook picked him out
From all of his neighbors
To make sauerkraut.

This is the moral
The story would show:
The softer you sing, why
The longer you'll grow.

Willie was an onion,
In the onion row,
But he was so lazy
He wouldn't grow.

Along came a cut-worm
One dark night;
Willie was so thin
He couldn't fight.

The moral is here:
Grow while you may
To fight the cut-worms
That come your way.

HELEN UNDERWOOD HOYT

THE WIND

The wind is such an optimist
    That we can learn from him
How we can turn into a tune
    A grief, however grim.

For even in a broken fence,
    A crack, however long,
Will make him pucker up his lips
    And whistle through a song!

        LOUIS GINSBERG

PROVERBS

Good Advice

Don't shirk
Your work
For the sake of a dream;
A fish
In the dish
Is worth ten in the stream.

Lesson from a Sun-dial

Ignore dull days; forget the showers;
Keep count of only shining hours.

Motto

However they talk, whatever they say,
Look straight at the task without dismay—
And if you can do it, do it today.

Day-dreamer

Too much thought:
Too little wrought.

Short Sermon

To give—and forgive—
Is a good way to live.

Thanks

To thank with a phrase
Is not worthy of praise.

To thank with the heart
Is the better part.

To thank with a fact—
Act.

FROM THE GERMAN
Adapted by Louis Untermeyer

THE BEST FIRM

A pretty good firm is "Watch & Waite,"
And another is "Attit, Early & Layte";
And still another is "Doo & Dairit";
But the best is probably "Grinn & Barrett."

WALTER G. DOTY

GRACE FOR A CHILD

Here a little child I stand,
Heaving up my either hand;
Cold as paddocks though they be,
Here I lift them up to Thee,
For a benison to fall
On our meat and on us all.
                    Amen.

ROBERT HERRICK

AN ANGEL SINGING

I heard an Angel singing
When the day was springing,
"Mercy, Pity, Peace
Is the world's release."

Thus he sung all day
Over the new mown hay,
Till the sun went down
And haycocks looked brown.

WILLIAM BLAKE

461

THINGS TO REMEMBER

A robin redbreast in a cage
Puts all Heaven in a rage.

A skylark wounded on the wing,
A cherubim does cease to sing.

He who shall hurt the little wren
Shall never be beloved by men.

The wanton boy that kills the fly
Shall feel the spider's enmity.

A truth that's told with bad intent
Beats all the lies you can invent.

WILLIAM BLAKE

BY MYSELF

Let me be the one
To do what is done.

ROBERT FROST

THE RAINBOW

The rainbow arches in the sky,
But in the earth it ends;
And if you ask the reason why,
They'll tell you "That depends."

It never comes without the rain,
Nor goes without the sun;
And though you try with might and main,
You'll never catch me one.

Perhaps you'll see it once a year,
Perhaps you'll say: "No, twice";
But every time it does appear,
It's very clean and nice.

If I were God, I'd like to win
At sun-and-moon croquet:
I'd drive the rainbow-wickets in
And ask someone to play.

DAVID MC CORD

RAINBOW IN THE SKY

My heart leaps up when I behold
   A rainbow in the sky:
So was it when my life began;
So is it now I am a man;
So be it when I shall grow old,
   Or let me die!

                WILLIAM WORDSWORTH

ACKNOWLEDGMENTS

MANY of the verses in this volume are so new that they have never before appeared in print; many of them are older than the memory of any living man. Several of the more recent, however, have been published in books of our own time, and especial acknowledgment must be made to them. I wish to thank not only the poets who have helped me make this collection, but the publishers who are holders of the copyrights and whose permission to quote from their books has been of such assistance. Alphabetically speaking, they are as follows:

D. Appleton-Century Company—for "The Pepper Tree" from *Knights Errant* by Sister M. Madeleva.

Curtis Brown, Ltd.—for the poems by Beatrice Curtis Brown, originally published in *Child Life*.

Coward-McCann, Inc.—for "The Mouse" from *Compass Rose* by Elizabeth Coatsworth, copyright, 1929, by Coward-McCann, Inc.

Doubleday, Doran & Company, Inc.—for "Yesterday in Oxford Street" from *Fairies and Chimneys* by Rose Fyleman, copyright, 1920, by Doubleday, Doran & Company, Inc.

Dodd, Mead & Company—for the selections from *Mixed Beasts* by Kenyon Cox.

The Hampshire Bookshop—for the selections from *Bramble-Fruit* by Helen Underwood Hoyt.

Harcourt, Brace and Company, Inc.—for "The Day of the Circus Horse" from *Carmina* by T. A. Daly, the quotations from *Selected Poems* by W. H. Davies, "Chairoplane Chant," "The Resolute Cat," "Prince Peter," and "The Little Road" from *Magpie Lane* by Nancy Byrd Turner, copyright, 1927; for "The Willow Cats" from *Little Girl and Boy Land* by Margaret Widdemer, copyright, 1924; for "Jewish Lullaby" from *Burning Bush* by Louis Untermeyer, copyright, 1928, all of which are used by per-

Acknowledgments

mission of, and by special arrangement with, Harcourt, Brace and Company, Inc.

HENRY HOLT AND COMPANY—for "To the Thawing Wind" from *A Boy's Will* by Robert Frost; for "The Three Beggars," "As Lucy Went a-Walking" from *Down-Adown-Derry,* by Walter de la Mare and "Jim Jay" from *Peacock Pie* by Walter de la Mare, all of which are used by permission of, and by special arrangement with, Henry Holt and Company.

HOUGHTON MIFFLIN COMPANY—for "The Deacon's Masterpiece" from *Complete Poetical Works of Oliver Wendell Holmes,* the selections from "Hiawatha's Childhood," "Rain in Summer," "Paul Revere's Ride," and "The Secret of the Sea" from *The Complete Works of Henry Wadsworth Longfellow,* "Evening at the Farm" from *The Poetical Works of John Townsend Trowbridge* and "Barbara Frietchie" from *The Complete Poetical Works of John Greenleaf Whittier,* all of which are used by permission of, and by special arrangement with, Houghton Mifflin Company, the authorized publishers.

CLAUDE KENDALL—for the selections from *Funday* and *Father Gander* by Ilo Orleans.

ALFRED A. KNOPF, INC.—for the selections from *The Bad Child's Book of Beasts* and *Cautionary Tales for Children* by Hilaire Belloc, and for the poem from *Gay and Wistful* by Newman Levy, reprinted by permission of, and by special arrangement with, Alfred A. Knopf, Inc., authorized publishers.

LITTLE, BROWN AND COMPANY—for "A Legend of Lake Okeefinokee," "Little John Bottlejohn," "Nonsense Verses," and "Emily Jane" from *Tirra Lirra* by Laura E. Richards, and "A fuzzy fellow without feet" from *The Complete Poems of Emily Dickinson.*

THE MACMILLAN COMPANY—for "Song of the Rabbits Outside of the Window" from *Away Goes Sally* by Elizabeth Coatsworth.

A. C. McCLURG AND COMPANY—for the selections from *When Little Boys Sing* by John and Rue Carpenter.

G. P. PUTNAM'S SONS—MINTON, BALCH & COMPANY—for "Hiding" from *Everything and Anything* by Dorothy Aldis, for "Winter Coats," "What

Am I?" and "The Harpers' Farm" from *Hop! Skip! and Jump!* by Dorothy Aldis.

JOSEPH SARGENT, Administrator of the estate of Guy Wetmore Carryl—for "How the Babes in the Wood Showed They Couldn't Be Beaten" from *Grimm Tales Made Gay.*

THE SATURDAY REVIEW OF LITERATURE—for "When I was Christened," "Tiggady Rue," and "The Frost Pane" by David McCord, and "Song of the Rabbits Outside the Tavern" by Elizabeth Coatsworth.

G. SCHIRMER, INC.—for the verses from *Improving Songs for Anxious Children* by John Alden and Rue Carpenter.

CHARLES SCRIBNER's SONS—for "The Dog" from *The Kitten's Garden of Verses* by Oliver Herford, for "The Rock-a-By Lady," "Seein' Things" and "The Doll's Wooing" from *The Collected Poems of Eugene Field.*

RICHARD R. SMITH, INC.—for "Morning at the Beach" from *Songs for Johnny-Jump-Up* by John Farrar.

THE VIKING PRESS—for "Milking Time" and "The Picnic" from *Under the Tree* by Elizabeth Madox Roberts.

YALE UNIVERSITY PRESS—for "Serious Omission" from *Songs for Parents* by John Farrar.

I am personally indebted to Violet Underwood Hoyt for consent to reprint the selections from *Bramble-Fruit* by her daughter, Helen Underwood Hoyt, and to Joseph Sargent, administrator of the estate of Guy Wetmore Carryl, for permission to reprint Carryl's "How the Babes in the Wood Showed They Couldn't Be Beaten" from *Grimm Tales Made Gay,* now, unfortunately, out of print.

My thanks are also due and gratefully tendered to Robert Frost, David McCord, Elizabeth Coatsworth, John Alden Carpenter, Edwin Markham, Ilo Orleans, Eleanor Farjeon, Laura E. Richards, Merrill Moore, Louis Ginsberg, Beatrice Curtis Brown, Carolyn Hancock, Emma Rounds, William Sargent, Robin Christopher (A. B. Shiffrin), Molly Michaels, Joseph Lauren, Michael Lewis, and Esther Antin, whose personal cooperation has been invaluable, permitting me, in many instances, to quote

Acknowledgments

poems not yet published in any of their volumes, several of the verses never having hitherto appeared in print.

If any verses are not specifically acknowledged it is an oversight, an oversight which will be corrected if readers will call attention to the omission of credit.

I am likewise grateful to Helen Grace Carlisle, Catherine McCarthy, and Marion Darragh, whose keen memories recaptured many of the game-rhymes and counting-out verses. Since most of these jingles have never (as far as I know) achieved the dignity of the printed page, the various versions differ surprisingly. Whenever I have been undecided which version is closest to the uncertain original, whether to publish a favored line as, say,

> Walter, Walter, wine-flower

or

> Water, water, wildflower

theirs have been the deciding voices.

Finally, I must thank my willing friends and reluctant critics, especially one Alexander Lindey, two Moores (Merrill and Ann Leslie), and five Brewsters (Gregory, Martha, Jane, Patricia, and Nancy) for being the creative listeners they are.

INDEX OF AUTHORS

INDEX OF TITLES

INDEX OF FIRST LINES

INDEX OF AUTHORS

Index of Authors

Index of Authors

Index of Authors

Index of Authors

INDEX OF TITLES

Index of Titles

Index of Titles

Index of Titles

Index of Titles

Index of Titles

Index of Titles

Index of Titles

Index of Titles

Index of Titles

Index of Titles

Index of Titles

INDEX OF FIRST LINES

Index of First Lines

Index of First Lines

Index of First Lines

495

Index of First Lines

Index of First Lines